I0632450

TOGETHER IN PEACE

BX 2260 .C42 1975

TOGETHER IN PEACE

by

Joseph M. Champlin

WITHDRAWN

ST. FRANCIS SEMINARY
SALZMANN
LIBRARY
Milwaukee, Wis. 53207

AVE MARIA PRESS
NOTRE DAME, INDIANA 46556

FATHER JOSEPH M. CHAMPLIN, former Associate Director, Secretariat, Bishops' Committee on the Liturgy, is Pastor of Holy Family Church, Fulton, New York. He has lectured extensively throughout the country, and his syndicated column appears in 90 Catholic newspapers.

His other works include *Together For Life,* the most popular marriage preparation book in use today (over a million copies in print), *Don't You Really Love Me?* (200,000 in print), *Christ Present And Yet To Come, The Mass In a World of Change,* and *The Sacraments In a World of Change.* In addition, he has appeared on national radio and television, and has recorded several cassettes on liturgy and pastoral life.

First Printing: 25,000

Nihil Obstat: Rev. John L. Roark
　　　　　　　 Censor Deputatus
　　　　　　　 August 22, 1974

Imprimatur: Most Rev. David F. Cunningham, D.D.
　　　　　　　 Bishop of Syracuse

Acknowledgments

Text of *The New American Bible* used by license of the Confraternity of Christian Doctrine, Washington, D.C.

English translation of the *Rite of Penance,* copyright © 1974, International Committee on English in the Liturgy, Inc. All rights reserved.

ISBN: 0-87793-094-5

Copyright 1975 by Ave Maria Press. All rights reserved

Photography: Larry Hoyt

Printed in the United States of America

For the priests and penitents
in my life who have sought or
given Christ's healing peace

Contents

PART III: THE RITE OF PENANCE

PART I
Penitent's Section

Introduction

God has given us the sacrament of Penance so troubled sinners might meet with faith the forgiving Jesus Christ and walk away in peace.

The stronger our faith, the clearer we view our sins, the more honestly we confess them, the greater our desire to improve, the deeper will be the inner joy and personal freedom we experience on those occasions.

This booklet is designed to help in each of these areas. You may follow the text by yourself or together with a priest who wishes to share portions of it with his penitents.

There are five steps which surround and make possible a peaceful meeting with the Lord of mercy. The sections of this book correspond to each of those stages.

Step 1:
Prayer for Light and Courage

We begin by a brief prayer asking God to help us believe in his mercy, to see our sins just as they are, to confess them honestly despite the pain that involves, to experience his peace, and to change our future lives.

This prayer from the heart can be in your own words and thoughts or may be expressed in one of the formulas below:

A.

God our Father in heaven,
send your Holy Spirit into my heart.
Point out my sins.
Supply the courage I need to confess them honestly.
Help me to believe you are always willing to forgive.
Remove my sin and guilt,
fill me with peace,
then send me away strong, free,
and determined I will be better in the days ahead.
I ask for these things through Jesus, your Son,
who is my Lord and Savior.

B. PSALM 6

I

O LORD, reprove me not in your anger,
  nor chastise me in your wrath.
Have pity on me, O LORD, for I am languishing;
  heal me, O LORD, for my body is in terror;
My soul, too, is utterly terrified;
  but you, O LORD, how long . . . ?

II

Return, O LORD, save my life;
  rescue me because of your kindness,
For among the dead no one remembers you;
  in the nether world who gives you thanks?

III

I am wearied with sighing;
  every night I flood my bed with weeping;
  I drench my couch with my tears.
My eyes are dimmed with sorrow;
  they have aged because of all my foes.

IV

Depart from me, all evildoers,
  for the LORD has heard the sound of my weeping;
The LORD has heard my plea;
  the LORD has accepted my prayer.
All my enemies shall be put to shame in utter terror;
  they shall fall back in sudden shame.

C. PSALM 38

I

O LORD, in your anger punish me not,
  in your wrath chastise me not;
For your arrows have sunk deep in me,
  and your hand has come down upon me.
There is no health in my flesh because of your
    indignation;
  there is no wholeness in my bones because of
    my sin,

For my iniquities have overwhelmed me;
  they are like a heavy burden, beyond my strength.

II

Noisome and festering are my sores
  because of my folly,
I am stooped and bowed down profoundly;
  all the day I go in mourning,
For my loins are filled with burning pains;
  there is no health in my flesh.
I am numbed and severely crushed;
  I roar with anguish of heart.

O LORD, all my desire is before you;
  from you my groaning is not hid.
My heart throbs; my strength forsakes me;
  the very light of my eyes has failed me.
My friends and my companions stand back because of
    my affliction;
  my neighbors stand afar off.
Men lay snares for me seeking my life;
  they look to my misfortune, they speak of ruin,
  treachery they talk of all the day.

III

But I am like a deaf man, hearing not,
  like a dumb man who opens not his mouth.
I am become like a man who neither hears
  nor has in his mouth a retort.
Because for you, O LORD, I wait;
  you, O Lord my God, will answer
When I say, "Let them not be glad on my account
  who, when my foot slips, glory over me."

For I am very near to falling,
  and my grief is with me always.
Indeed, I acknowledge my guilt;
  I grieve over my sin.
But my undeserved enemies are strong;
  many are my foes without cause.
Those who repay evil for good
  harass me for pursuing good.
Forsake me not, O LORD;
  my God, be not far from me!
Make haste to help me,
  O Lord my salvation!

D. PSALM 130

I

Out of the depths I cry to you, O LORD;
  Lord, hear my voice!
Let your ears be attentive
  to my voice in supplication:

II

If you, O LORD, mark iniquities,
  Lord, who can stand?
But with you is forgiveness,
  that you may be revered.

III

I trust in the LORD;
  my soul trusts in his word.
My soul waits for the LORD
  more than sentinels wait for the dawn.

IV

More than sentinels wait for the dawn,
   let Israel wait for the LORD,
For with the LORD is kindness
   and with him is plenteous redemption;
And he will redeem
   Israel from all their iniquities.

Step 2:
God's Good Words About Forgiveness

The bible is filled with stories and teachings about God's limitless mercy, love and forgiveness. Read now one or a few of the selections below and reflect for several moments upon them.

A. Matthew 9:9-13 *Jesus' Concern for Sinners*

As he moved on, Jesus saw a man named Matthew at his post where taxes were collected. He said to him, "Follow me." Matthew got up and followed him. Now it happened that, while Jesus was at table in Matthew's home, many tax collectors and those known as sinners came to join Jesus and his disciples at dinner. The Pharisees saw this and complained to his disciples, "What reason can the Teacher have for eating with tax collectors and those who disregard the law?" Overhearing the remark, he said: "People who are in good health do not need a doctor; sick people do. Go and learn the meaning of the words, 'It is mercy I desire and not sacrifice.' I have come to call, not the self-righteous, but sinners."

B. Luke 5:17-26 *Christ Forgives and Cures the Paralytic*

One day Jesus was teaching, and the power of the Lord made him heal. Sitting close by were Pharisees and teachers of the law who had come from every village of Galilee and from Judea and Jerusalem.

Some men came along carrying a paralytic on a mat. They were trying to bring him in and lay him before Jesus; but they found no way of getting him through because of the crowd, so they went up on the roof. There they let him down with his mat through the tiles into the middle of the crowd before Jesus. Seeing their faith, Jesus said, "My friend, your sins are forgiven you."

The scribes and the Pharisees began a discussion, saying: "Who is this man who utters blasphemies? Who can forgive sins but God alone?" Jesus, however, knew their reasoning and answered them by saying: "Why do you harbor these thoughts? Which is easier: to say, 'Your sins are forgiven you,' or to say, 'Get up and walk'? In any case, to make it clear to you that the Son of Man has authority on earth to forgive sins"—he then addressed the paralyzed man: "I say to you, get up! Take your mat with you, and return to your house."

At once the man stood erect before them. He picked up the mat he had been lying on and went home praising God. At this they were all seized with astonishment. Full of awe, they gave praise to God, saying, "We have seen incredible things today!"

C. Luke 7:36-50 *The Lord and a Penitent Woman*

There was a certain Pharisee who invited Jesus to dine with him. Jesus went to the Pharisee's home and reclined to eat. A woman known in the town to be a sinner learned that he was dining in the Pharisee's home. She brought in a vase of perfumed oil and stood behind him at his feet, weeping so that her tears fell upon his feet. Then she wiped them with her hair, kissing them and perfuming them with the oil. When his host, the Pharisee, saw this, he said to himself, "If this man were a prophet, he would

16

know who and what sort of woman this is that touches him—that she is a sinner." In answer to his thoughts, Jesus said to him, "Simon, I have something to propose to you." "Teacher," he said, "speak."

"Two men owed money to a certain money-lender; one owed a total of five hundred coins, the other fifty. Since neither was able to repay, he wrote off both debts. Which of them was more grateful to him?" Simon answered, "He, I presume, to whom he remitted the larger sum." Jesus said to him, "You are right."

Turning then to the woman, he said to Simon: "You see this woman? I came to your home and you provided me with no water for my feet. She has washed my feet with her tears and wiped them with her hair. You gave me no kiss, but she has not ceased kissing my feet since I entered. You did not anoint my head with oil, but she has anointed my feet with perfume. I tell you, that is why her many sins are forgiven—because of her great love. Little is forgiven the one whose love is small."

He said to her then, "Your sins are forgiven"; at which his fellow guests began to ask among themselves, "Who is this that he even forgives sins?" Meanwhile he said to the woman, "Your faith has been your salvation. Now go in peace."

D. Luke 15:1-7 *A Story of the Lost Sheep*

The tax collectors and sinners were all gathering around to hear him, at which the Pharisees and the scribes murmured, "This man welcomes sinners and eats with them." Then he addressed this parable to them: "Who among you, if he has a hundred sheep and loses one of them, does not leave the ninety-nine in the wasteland and follow the lost one until he finds it? And when he finds it, he puts it on his

17

shoulders in jubilation. Once arrived home, he invites friends and neighbors in and says to them, 'Rejoice with me because I have found my lost sheep.' I tell you, there will likewise be more joy in heaven over one repentant sinner than over ninety-nine righteous people who have no need to repent.

E. Luke 15:8-10 *The Misplaced Silver Coin*

"What woman, if she has ten silver pieces and loses one, does not light a lamp and sweep the house in a diligent search until she has retrieved what she lost? And when she finds it, she calls in her friends and neighbors to say, 'Rejoice with me! I have found the silver piece I lost.' I tell you, there will be the same kind of joy before the angels of God over one repentant sinner."

F. Luke 15:11-32 *The Wandering and Wasteful Son Who Returned Home*

Jesus said to them: "A man had two sons. The younger of them said to his father, 'Father, give me the share of the estate that is coming to me.' So the father divided up the property. Some days later this younger son collected all his belongings and went off to a distant land, where he squandered his money on dissolute living. After he had spent everything, a great famine broke out in that country and he was in dire need. So he attached himself to one of the propertied class of the place, who sent him to his farm to take care of the pigs. He longed to fill his belly with the husks that were fodder for the pigs, but no one made a move to give him anything. Coming to his senses at last, he said: 'How many hired hands at my father's place have more than enough to eat, while here I am starving! I will break away and return to

18

my father, and say to him, Father, I have sinned against God and against you; I no longer deserve to be called your son. Treat me like one of your hired hands.' With that he set off for his father's house. While he was still a long way off, his father caught sight of him and was deeply moved. He ran out to meet him, threw his arms around his neck, and kissed him. The son said to him, 'Father, I have sinned against God and against you; I no longer deserve to be called your son.' The father said to his servants: 'Quick! bring out the finest robe and put it on him; put a ring on his finger and shoes on his feet. Take the fatted calf and kill it. Let us eat and celebrate, because this son of mine was dead and has come back to life. He was lost and is found.' Then the celebration began.

"Meanwhile the elder son was out on the land. As he neared the house on his way home, he heard the sound of music and dancing. He called one of the servants and asked him the reason for the dancing and the music. The servant answered, 'Your brother is home, and your father has killed the fatted calf because he has him back in good health.' The son grew angry at this and would not go in; but his father came out and began to plead with him.

"He said to his father in reply: 'For years now I have slaved for you. I never disobeyed one of your orders, yet you never gave me so much as a kid goat to celebrate with my friends. Then, when this son of yours returns after having gone through your property with loose women, you kill the fatted calf for him.'

"'My son,' replied the father, 'you are with me always, and everything I have is yours. But we had to celebrate and rejoice! This brother of yours was dead, and has come back to life. He was lost, and is found.'"

G. Luke 19:1-10 *Jesus and Zacchaeus the Tax Collector*

Entering Jericho, he passed through the city. There was a man there named Zacchaeus, the chief tax collector and a wealthy man. He was trying to see what Jesus was like, but being small of stature, was unable to do so because of the crowd. He first ran on in front, then climbed a sycamore tree which was along Jesus' route, in order to see him. When Jesus came to the spot he looked up and said, "Zacchaeus, hurry down. I mean to stay at your house today." He quickly descended, and welcomed him with delight. When this was observed, everyone began to murmur, "He has gone to a sinner's house as a guest."

Zacchaeus stood his ground and said to the Lord: "I give half my belongings, Lord, to the poor. If I have defrauded anyone in the least, I pay him back fourfold." Jesus said to him: "Today salvation has come to this house, for this is what it means to be a son of Abraham. The Son of Man has come to search out and save what was lost."

H. John 8:1-11 *A Woman Caught in Adultery*

Then each went off to his own house, while Jesus went out to the Mount of Olives. At daybreak he reappeared in the temple area; and when the people started coming to him, he sat down and began to teach them. The scribes and the Pharisees led a woman forward who had been caught in adultery. They made her stand in front of everyone. "Teacher," they said to him, "this woman has been caught in the act of adultery. In the law, Moses ordered such women to be stoned. What do you have to say about the case?" (They were posing this question to trap him, so that they could have something to accuse him of.) Jesus bent down and started tracing on the ground with his finger. When they persisted in their questioning, he straightened up and said to them, "Let the man among you who has no sin be the first to cast a stone at her." A second time he bent down and wrote on the ground. Then the audience drifted away one by one, beginning with the elders. This left him alone with the woman, who continued to stand there before him. Jesus finally straightened up and said to her, "Woman, where did they all disappear to? Has no one condemned you?" "No one, sir," she answered. Jesus said, "Nor do I condemn you. You may go. But from now on, avoid this sin."

I. John 20:19-23 *Christ's Easter Gift of Peace and Forgiveness*

On the evening of that first day of the week, even though the disciples had locked the doors of the place where they were for fear of the Jews, Jesus came and stood before them. "Peace be with you," he said. When he had said this, he showed them his hands and his side. At the sight of the Lord the disciples rejoiced. "Peace be with you," he said again.

"As the Father has sent me, so I send you." Then he breathed on them and said: "Receive the Holy Spirit. If you forgive men's sins, they are forgiven them; if you hold them bound, they are held bound."

J. Romans 5:6-11 *The Lord Died for Our Sins*

At the appointed time, when we were still powerless, Christ died for us godless men. It is rare that anyone should lay down his life for a just man, though it is barely possible that for a good man someone may have the courage to die. It is precisely in this that

21

God proves his love for us; that while we were still sinners, Christ died for us. Now that we have been justified by his blood, it is all the more certain that we shall be saved by him from God's wrath. For if, when we were God's enemies, we were reconciled to him by the death of his Son, it is all the more certain that we who have been reconciled will be saved by his life. Not only that; we go so far as to make God our boast through our Lord Jesus Christ, through whom we have now received reconciliation.

K. Isaiah 53:1-12 *An Old Testament Prediction of the Savior's Sufferings*

Who would believe what we have heard?
    To whom has the arm of the LORD been revealed?
He grew up like a sapling before him,
    like a shoot from the parched earth;
There was in him no stately bearing to make us look
        at him,
    nor appearance that would attract us to him.
He was spurned and avoided by men,
    a man of suffering, accustomed to infirmity,
One of those from whom men hide their faces,
    spurned, and we held him in no esteem.

Yet it was our infirmities that he bore.
    our sufferings that he endured,
While we thought of him as stricken,
    as one smitten by God and afflicted.
But he was pierced for our offenses,
    crushed for our sins;
Upon him was the chastisement that makes us whole,
    by his stripes we were healed.
We had all gone astray like sheep,
    each following his own way;
But the LORD laid upon him the guilt of us all.

Though he was harshly treated, he submitted
  and opened not his mouth;
Like a lamb led to the slaughter
  or a sheep before the shearers,
  he was silent and opened not his mouth.
Oppressed and condemned, he was taken away,
  and who would have thought any more of his
      destiny?
When he was cut off from the land of the living,
  and smitten for the sin of his people,
A grave was assigned him among the wicked
  and a burial place with evildoers,
Though he had done no wrong, nor spoken any
      falsehood.
[But the LORD was pleased to crush him in infirmity.]

If he gives his life as an offering for sin,
  he shall see his descendants in a long life,
and the will of the LORD shall be accomplished
      through him.

Because of his affliction he shall see the light in
      fullness of days;
Through his suffering, my servant shall justify many,
  and their guilt he shall bear.
Therefore I will give him his portion among the great,
  and he shall divide the spoils with the mighty,
Because he surrendered himself to death
  and was counted among the wicked;
And he shall take away the sins of many,
  and win pardon for their offenses.

L. Ezekiel 18:20-32 *The Converted Sinner Shall Live*

Only the one who sins shall die. The son shall not be
charged with the guilt of his father, nor shall the
father be charged with the guilt of his son. The
virtuous man's virtue shall be his own, as the wicked

23

man's wickedness shall be his.

But if the wicked man turns away from all the sins he committed, if he keeps all my statutes and does what is right and just, he shall surely live, he shall not die. None of the crimes he committed shall be remembered against him; he shall live because of the virtue he has practiced. Do I indeed derive any pleasure from the death of the wicked? says the Lord GOD. Do I not rather rejoice when he turns from his evil way that he may live?

And if the virtuous man turns from the path of virtue to do evil, the same kind of abominable things that the wicked man does, can he do this and still live? None of his virtuous deeds shall be remembered, because he has broken faith and committed sin; because of this, he shall die. You say, "The LORD's way is not fair!" Hear now, house of Israel: Is it my way that is unfair, or rather, are not your ways unfair? When a virtuous man turns away from virtue to commit iniquity, and dies, it is because of the iniquity he committed that he must die. But if a wicked man, turning from the wickedness he has committed, does what is right and just, he shall preserve his life; since he has turned away from all the sins which he committed, he shall surely live, he shall not die. And yet the house of Israel says, "The LORD's way is not fair!" Is it my way that is not fair, house of Israel, or rather, is it not that your ways are not fair?

Therefore I will judge you, house of Israel, each one according to his ways, says the Lord GOD. Turn and be converted from all your crimes, that they may be no cause of guilt for you. Cast away from you all the crimes you have committed, and make for yourselves a new heart and a new spirit. Why should you die, O house of Israel? For I have no pleasure in the death of anyone who dies, says the Lord GOD. Return and live!

M. Daniel 9:4-23 *The Confession of Daniel*

I prayed to the LORD, my God, and confessed,
"Ah, LORD, great and awesome God, you who keep
your merciful covenant toward those who love you
and observe your commandments! We have sinned,
been wicked and done evil; we have rebelled and
departed from your commandments and your laws.
We have not obeyed your servants the prophets, who
spoke in your name to our kings, our princes, our
fathers, and all the people of the land.
Justice, O Lord, is on your side; we are shamefaced
even to this day; the men of Judah, the residents of
Jerusalem, and all Israel, near and far, in all the
countries to which you have scattered them because
of their treachery toward you. O LORD, we are
shamefaced, like our kings, our princes, and our fathers,
for having sinned against you. But yours, O Lord, our
God, are compassion and forgiveness! Yet we rebelled
against you and paid no heed to your command,
O LORD, our God, to live by the law you gave us
through your servants the prophets. Because all Israel
transgressed your law and went astray, not heeding
your voice, the sworn malediction, recorded in the
law of Moses, the servant of God, was poured out over
us for our sins. You carried out the threats you spoke
against us and against those who governed us, by
bringing upon us in Jerusalem the greatest calamity
that has ever occurred under heaven. As it is written in
the law of Moses, this calamity came full upon us. As
we did not appease the LORD, our God, by turning
back from our wickedness and recognizing his
constancy, so the LORD kept watch over the calamity
and brought it upon us. You, O LORD, our God, are
just in all that you have done, for we did not listen to
your voice.
"Now, O Lord, our God, who led your people out

of the land of Egypt with a strong hand, and made a name for yourself even to this day, we have sinned, we are guilty. O Lord, in keeping with all your just deeds, let your anger and your wrath be turned away from your city Jerusalem, your holy mountain. On account of our sins and the crimes of our fathers, Jerusalem and your people have become the reproach of all our neighbors. Hear, therefore, O God, the prayer and petition of your servant; and for your own sake, O Lord, let your face shine upon your desolate sanctuary. Give ear, O my God, and listen; open your eyes and see our ruins and the city which bears your name. When we present our petition before you, we rely not on our just deeds, but on your great mercy. O Lord, hear! O Lord, pardon! O Lord, be attentive and act without delay, for your own sake, O my God, because this city and your people bear your name!"

I was still occupied with my prayer, confessing my sin and the sin of my people Israel, presenting my petition to the LORD, my God, on behalf of his holy mountain—I was still occupied with this prayer, when Gabriel, the one whom I had seen before in vision, came to me in rapid flight at the time of the evening sacrifice. He instructed me in these words: "Daniel, I have now come to give you understanding. When you began your petition, an answer was given which I have come to announce, because you are beloved. Therefore, mark the answer and understand the vision."

N. Isaiah 55:1-12 *The Mysterious Ways and Mercy of God*

All you who are thirsty,
    come to the water!
You who have no money,

come, receive grain and eat;
Come, without paying and without cost,
    drink wine and milk!
Why spend your money for what is not bread;
    your wages for what fails to satisfy?
Heed me, and you shall eat well,
    you shall delight in rich fare.
Come to me heedfully,
    listen, that you may have life.
I will renew with you the everlasting covenant,
    the benefits assured to David.
As I made him a witness to the peoples,
    a leader and commander of nations,
So shall you summon a nation you knew not,
    and nations that knew you not shall run to you,
Because of the Lord, your God,
    the Holy One of Israel, who has glorified you.

Seek the LORD while he may be found,
    call him while he is near.
Let the scoundrel forsake his way,
    and the wicked man his thoughts;
Let him turn to the LORD for mercy;
    to our God, who is generous in forgiving.
For my thoughts are not your thoughts,
    nor are your ways my ways, says the LORD.
As high as the heavens are above the earth,
    so high are my ways above your ways
    and my thoughts above your thoughts.

For just as from the heavens
    the rain and snow come down
And do not return there
    till they have watered the earth,
    making it fertile and fruitful,
Giving seed to him who sows
    and bread to him who eats,

So shall my word be
   that goes forth from my mouth;
It shall not return to me void,
   but shall do my will,
   achieving the end for which I sent it.
Yes, in joy you shall depart,
   in peace you shall be brought back;
Mountains and hills shall break out in song before you,
   and all the trees of the countryside shall clap their
      hands.

O. Ezekiel 34:11-16 *God Is the Good Shepherd*

For thus says the Lord GOD: I myself will look
after and tend my sheep. As a shepherd tends his
flock when he finds himself among his scattered sheep,
so will I tend my sheep. I will rescue them from
every place where they were scattered when it was
cloudy and dark. I will lead them out from among the
peoples and gather them from the foreign lands; I will
bring them back to their own country and pasture
them upon the mountains of Israel [in the land's
ravines and all its inhabited places]. In good pastures
will I pasture them, and on the mountain heights of
Israel shall be their grazing ground. There they shall
lie down on good grazing ground, and in rich pastures
shall they be pastured on the mountains of Israel. I
myself will pasture my sheep; I myself will give them
rest, says the Lord GOD. The lost I will seek out, the
strayed I will bring back, the injured I will bind up,
the sick I will heal [but the sleek and the strong I will
destroy], shepherding them rightly.

P. Joel 2:12-19 *A Call to Repent*

Yet even now, says the LORD,
   return to me with your whole heart,

with fasting, and weeping, and mourning;
Rend your hearts, not your garments,
  and return to the LORD, your God.
For gracious and merciful is he,
  slow to anger, rich in kindness,
  and relenting in punishment.
Perhaps he will again relent
  and leave behind him a blessing,
Offerings and libations
  for the LORD, your God.

Blow the trumpet in Zion!
  proclaim a fast,
  call an assembly;
Gather the people,
  notify the congregation;
Assemble the elders,
  gather the children
  and the infants at the breast;
Let the bridegroom quit his room,
  and the bride her chamber.
Between the porch and the altar
  let the priests, the ministers of the LORD, weep,
And say, "Spare, O Lord, your people,
  and make not your heritage a reproach,
  with the nations ruling over them!
Why should they say among the peoples,
  'Where is their God?' "

Then the Lord was stirred to concern for his land and
took pity on his people. The Lord answered and said to
his people:

See, I will send you grain, and wine, and oil
  and you shall be filled with them;
No more will I make you
  a reproach among the nations.

Q. Micah 7:2-7, 18-20 *Confidence in God's Mercy*

The faithful are gone from the earth,
  among men the upright are no more!
They all lie in wait to shed blood,
  each one ensnares the other.
Their hands succeed at evil;
  the prince makes demands,
The judge is had for a price,
  The great man speaks as he pleases,
The best of them is like a brier,
  the most upright like a thorn hedge.
The day announced by your watchmen!
  your punishment has come;
  now is the time of your confusion.
Put no trust in a friend,
  have no confidence in a companion;
Against her who lies in your bosom
  guard the portals of your mouth.
For the son dishonors his father,
  the daughter rises up against her mother,
The daughter-in-law against her mother-in-law,
  and a man's enemies are those of his household.
But as for me, I will look to the Lord,
  I will put my trust in God my savior;
  my God will hear me!

Who is there like you, the God who removes guilt
  and pardons sin for the remnant of his inheritance;
Who does not persist in anger forever,
  but delights rather in clemency,
And will again have compassion on us,
  treading underfoot our guilt?
You will cast into the depths of the sea
  all our sins;
You will show faithfulness to Jacob,
  and grace to Abraham,
As you have sworn to our fathers
  from days of old.

Step 3:
A Look Into the Heart

This step requires a period of reflection sufficient for you to look at the past (How long since you last received the sacrament?) and to search out your sins over that period.

Are there sins because of what you did or what you failed to do? What sinful failures can you recall in thought, word or deed?

Serious sins, i.e., major wrongs committed or omitted with full awareness and total freedom, will probably come quickly to your attention or already press heavily on your mind.

These should be confessed in this way: what you did (or failed to do), any major circumstances which notably change the kind of sin it was, and the approximate number of times.

Lesser sins need not be confessed. However, they are moral failures, too, and can be forgiven in the sacrament of Penance. Frankly confessing a few of them can help you conquer those faults and grow into the kind of person God wants you to become.

This reflective look at the past should be honest, down to earth, painful, but healthy and healing. Don't spend too long or dig too deeply; yet don't play games either or avoid coming to grips with what you know was wrong in the past.

A contemporary psychiatrist has this to say: "So long as a person lives under the shadow of real, unacknowledged, and unexpiated guilt, he . . . will continue to hate himself and to suffer the inevitable consequences of self-hatred. But the moment he . . . begins to accept his guilt and his sinfulness, the possibility of radical reformation opens up; and . . . a new freedom of self-respect and peace."[1]

If you would like some assistance here, the suggestions below may open up a few avenues of thought and lead to a better appreciation of what Jesus demands from his followers.

A. The Law of Love:

One of the scribes came up, and when he heard them arguing he realized how skillfully Jesus answered them. He decided to ask him, "Which is the first of all the commandments?" Jesus replied: "This is the first:

'Hear, O Israel! The Lord our God is Lord alone! Therefore you shall love the Lord your God

with all your heart,

with all your soul,

with all your mind,

and with all your strength.'

This is the second,

'You shall love your neighbor as yourself.'

There is no other commandment greater than these."
The scribe said to him: "Excellent, Teacher! You are right in saying, 'He is the One, there is no other than he.' Yes, 'to love him with all our heart, with all our thoughts and with all our strength, and to love our neighbor as ourselves' is worth more than any burnt offering or sacrifice." Jesus approved the insight of this answer and told him, "You are not far from the reign of God." And no one had the courage to ask him any more questions.—Mark 12:28-34

---

1. O. Hobart Mowrer, quoted in Karl Menninger's *Whatever Became of Sin?* Hawthorn Books, New York, 1973, p. 195.

Sin could well be spelled with a capital "I" in the middle. Sinful behavior is essentially selfish behavior. Sinners basically choose in a harmful, aggressive way the "I" over the "You" or seek someone, perhaps something, which is in fact self-destructive.

Love, on the contrary, is in its essence unselfish and self-giving.

Jesus' words to the scribe, then, present his followers with a simple, yet extremely taxing and personal guide for their lives.

That law of love taxes in an ongoing manner all our resources since it forms an ideal we never can reach, but merely strive to fulfill.

This commandment of Christ also takes on a highly personal character. Only I can judge if what I did or failed to do was selfish or not; and in some circumstances I am not even sure myself about the motivation behind certain actions or omissions.

The questions we ask at this point: Have I been selfish with regard to others? Have I chosen what I wanted, not what was best for me, and thus ultimately hurt myself in the process?

B. A Call to Holiness:

"In a word, you must be perfect as your heavenly Father is perfect." (Matthew 5:48)

If it has been many months or a few years since you last confessed your sins and you cannot think of anything at all to confess, this may be the moment to reflect on those words of Christ. Our Lord calls us to lead holy, perfect lives. If we have not seriously failed God, our neighbor or ourself, we could say wonderful, praise the Lord. But that is only a beginning step. Eliminating lesser sins, overcoming imperfections and putting on virtues detailed for us in the New Testament require a lifelong, uneven, often discouraging struggle. The victories and defeats in that effort are good subject matter for confession.

The story of a good man summoned by Jesus to become a better, perfect one follows.

As he was setting out on a journey a man came running up, knelt down before him and asked, "Good Teacher, what must I do to share in everlasting life?" Jesus answered, "Why do you call me good? No one is good but God alone. You know the commandments:
   'You shall not kill;
   You shall not commit adultery;
   You shall not steal;
   You shall not bear false witness;
   You shall not defraud;
   Honor your father and your mother.' "

He replied, "Teacher, I have kept all these since my childhood." Then Jesus looked at him with love and told him, "There is one thing more you must do. Go and sell what you have and give to the poor; you will then have treasure in heaven. After that, come and follow me." At these words the man's face fell. He went away sad, for he had many possessions. Jesus looked around and said to his disciples, "How hard it is for the rich to enter the kingdom of God!" The disciples could only marvel at his words. So Jesus repeated what he had said: "My sons, how hard it is to enter the kingdom of God! It is easier for a camel to pass through a needle's eye than for a rich man to enter the kingdom of God."

They were completely overwhelmed at this, and exclaimed to one another, "Then who can be saved?" —Mark 10:17-26

C. Triple Effects of Sin:

Sin destroys or weakens our friendship with God, ruins or hinders our relationships with others, and upsets the beauty or harmony of the world around us.

To repent, to change our hearts and ways involves a healing of these three wounds. We need to be reconciled with the Lord, with our neighbor and with the environment.

The book of Genesis, in its classic, poetic account of man's fall, describes those triple effects of sin: Adam and Eve lost God's special friendship, found their mutual relationships impaired (he blamed her; one of their children murdered the other), and witnessed the destruction of nature's peaceful pattern.

Now the serpent was the most cunning of all the animals that the LORD God had made. The serpent asked the woman, "Did God really tell you not to eat from any of the trees in the garden?" The woman answered the serpent: "We may eat of the fruit of the trees in the garden; it is only about the fruit of the tree in the middle of the garden that God said, 'You shall not eat it or even touch it, lest you die.'" But the serpent said to the woman: "You certainly will not die! No, God knows well that the moment you eat of it your eyes will be opened and you will be like gods who know what is good and what is bad." The woman saw that the tree was good for food, pleasing to the eyes, and desirable for gaining wisdom. So she took some of its fruit and ate it; and she also gave some to her husband, who was with her, and he ate it. Then the eyes of both of them were opened, and they realized that they were naked; so they sewed fig leaves together and made loincloths for themselves.
When they heard the sound of the LORD God moving about in the garden at the breezy time of the day, the man and his wife hid themselves from the LORD God among the trees of the garden. The LORD God then called to the man and asked him, "Where are you?" He answered, "I heard you in the garden;

but I was afraid, because I was naked, so I hid myself."
Then he asked, "Who told you that you were naked?
You have eaten, then, from the tree of which I had
forbidden you to eat!" The man replied, "The
woman whom you put here with me—she gave me
fruit from the tree, and so I ate it." The LORD God
then asked the woman, "Why did you do such a
thing?" The woman answered, "The serpent tricked
me into it, so I ate it."

Then the LORD God said to the serpent:

"Because you have done this, you shall be banned
    from all the animals
    and from all the wild creatures;
On your belly shall you crawl
    and dirt shall you eat
    all the days of your life.
I will put enmity between you and the woman,
    and between your offspring and hers;
He will strike at your head,
    while you strike at his heel."

To the woman he said:
"I will intensify the pangs of your childbearing;
    in pain shall you bring forth children.
Yet your urge shall be for your husband,
    and he shall be your master."

To the man he said: "Because you listened to your
wife and ate from the tree of which I had forbidden
you to eat,

    "Cursed be the ground because of you!
In toil shall you eat its yield all the days of your life.
Thorns and thistles shall it bring forth to you,
    as you eat of the plants of the field.
By the sweat of your face

cription of the last judgment which fol-
oth reassure our hearts and, at the same
us uneasy. It preaches that God remembers
sions when we recognized Christ in our
ghbor and responded accordingly; it also
at the Lord recalls those situations when we
see Jesus in troubled persons and neglected

rtunately few, if any of us, can come up with
t score on this test. Think of several partic-
fficult cases—the confused patient in a nursing
the emotionally or mentally disturbed, the
rebellious youngster, the "con" artist who seeks
out, the constantly imposing neighbor or rela-
e alcoholic, the unpleasant personnel at work—
dge yourself according to the gospel standards.

n the Son of Man comes in his glory, escorted
the angels of heaven, he will sit upon his royal
e, and all the nations will be assembled before
Then he will separate them into two groups,
shepherd separates sheep from goats. The sheep
will place on his right hand, the goats on his left.
king will say to those on his right: 'Come. You
e my Father's blessing! Inherit the kingdom pre-
red for you from the creation of the world. For
was hungry and you gave me food, I was thirsty
d you gave me drink. I was a stranger and you
elcomed me, naked and you clothed me. I was ill
nd you comforted me, in prison and you came to
isit me.' Then the just will ask him: 'Lord, when did
we see you hungry and feed you or see you thirsty
and give you drink? When did we welcome you away
from home or clothe you in your nakedness? When
did we visit you when you were ill or in prison?' The
king will answer them: 'I assure you, as often as you

shall you get bread to eat,
Until you return to the ground,
    from which you were taken;
For you are dirt,
    and to dirt you shall return."—Genesis 3:1-19

The man had relations with his wife Eve, and she conceived and bore Cain, saying, "I have produced a man with the help of the LORD." Next she bore his brother Abel. Abel became a keeper of flocks, and Cain a tiller of the soil. In the course of time Cain brought an offering to the LORD from the fruit of the soil, while Abel, for his part, brought one of the best firstlings of his flock. The LORD looked with favor on Abel and his offering, but on Cain and his offering he did not. Cain greatly resented this and was crest-fallen. So the LORD said to Cain: "Why are you so resentful and crestfallen? If you do well, you can hold up your head; but if not, sin is a demon lurking at the door: his urge is toward you, yet you can be his master."

Cain said to his brother Abel, "Let us go out in the field." When they were in the field, Cain attacked his brother Abel and killed him. Then the LORD asked Cain, "Where is your brother Abel?" He an-swered, "I do not know. Am I my brother's keeper?" The LORD then said: "What have you done! Listen: your brother's blood cries out to me from the soil! Therefore you shall be banned from the soil that opened its mouth to receive your brother's blood from your hand. If you till the soil, it shall no longer give you its produce. You shall become a restless wanderer on the earth." Cain said to the LORD: "My punish-ment is too great to bear. Since you have now banished me from the soil, and I must avoid your presence and become a restless wanderer on the earth, anyone may kill me at sight." "Not so!" the

LORD said to him. "If anyone kills Cain, Cain shall be avenged sevenfold." So the LORD put a mark on Cain, lest anyone should kill him at sight.
—Genesis 4:1-15

D. The Bare Minimum:

The ten commandments give us good guidelines for our lives. There would be peace on earth, if every person kept these divine rules. Yet the Christian is summoned higher and asked to move beyond those laws.

They form, then, a kind of bare minimum. If we have violated them, we know our lives have slipped below the danger point and certainly cannot call ourselves good Christians. That title is reserved for those who keep these precepts which follow *and* faithfully pursue the course Jesus sketched for us by his life and teaching.

Then God delivered all these commandments:

"I, the LORD, am your God, who brought you out of the land of Egypt, that place of slavery. You shall not have other gods besides me. You shall not carve idols for yourselves in the shape of anything in the sky above or on the earth below or in the waters beneath the earth; you shall not bow down before them or worship them. For I, the LORD, your God, am a jealous God, inflicting punishment for their fathers' wickedness on the children of those who hate me, down to the third and fourth generation; but bestowing mercy down to the thousandth generation, on the children of those who love me and keep my commandments.

"You shall not take the name of the LORD, your God, in vain. For the LORD will not leave unpunished him who takes his name in vain.

"Remember to k
days you may labor a
seventh day is the sab
No work may be done
son or daughter, or you
beast, or by the alien wh
the LORD made the hea
and all that is in them; bu
rested. That is why the LO
day and made it holy.

"Honor your father and
may have a long life in the la
your God, is giving you.

"You shall not kill.

"You shall not commit adul

"You shall not steal.

"You shall not bear false wit
neighbor.

"You shall not covet your neig
shall not covet your neighbor's wife
female slave, nor his ox or ass, nor a
belongs to him."

When the people witnessed the t
lightning, the trumpet blast and the m
they all feared and trembled. So they
position much farther away and said to
speak to us, and we will listen; but let n
to us, or we shall die." Moses answered
"Do not be afraid, for God has come to y
test you and put his fear upon you, lest yo
sin." Still the people remained at a distanc
Moses approached the cloud where God w
Exodus 20:1-21

E. Service o

The des
lows can b
time, leave
those occa
needy nei
teaches th
failed to
them.
Unfo
a perfec
ularly di
home,
deeply
a hand
tive, th
and ju

"Wh
by al
thro
him
as a
he
Th
ha
pa
I
a
v
a

did it for one of my least brothers, you did it for me.'

"Then he will say to those on his left: 'Out of my sight, you condemned, into that everlasting fire prepared for the devil and his angels! I was hungry and you gave me no food, I was thirsty and you gave me no drink. I was away from home and you gave me no welcome, naked and you gave me no clothing. I was ill and in prison and you did not come to comfort me.' Then they in turn will ask: 'Lord, when did we see you hungry or thirsty or away from home or naked, or ill or in prison and not attend you in your needs?' He will answer them: 'I assure you, as often as you neglected to do it to one of these least ones, you neglected to do it to me.' These will go off to eternal punishment and the just to eternal life."
—Matthew 25:31-46

F. Misusing Ourselves and Others:

St. Paul in several places takes the ideal law of love and applies it to very specific circumstances.

My brothers, remember that you have been called to live in freedom—but not a freedom that gives free rein to the flesh. Out of love, place yourselves at one another's service. The whole law has found its fulfillment in this one saying: "You shall love your neighbor as yourself." If you go on biting and tearing one another to pieces, take care! You will end up in mutual destruction!

My point is that you should live in accord with the spirit and you will not yield to the cravings of the flesh. The flesh lusts against the spirit and the spirit against the flesh; the two are directly opposed. This is why you do not do what your will intends. If you are guided by the spirit, you are not under the law. It is obvious what proceeds from the flesh: lewd

41

conduct, impurity, licentiousness, idolatry, sorcery, hostilities, bickering, jealousy, outbursts of rage, selfish rivalries, dissensions, factions, envy, drunkenness, orgies, and the like. I warn you, as I have warned you before: those who do such things will not inherit the kingdom of God!

In contrast, the fruit of the spirit is love, joy, peace, patient endurance, kindness, generosity, faith, mildness, and chastity. Against such there is no law! Those who belong to Christ Jesus have crucified their flesh with its passions and desires. Since we live by the spirit, let us follow the spirit's lead. Let us never be boastful, or challenging, or jealous toward one another.—Galatians 5:13-26

Be imitators of God as his dear children. Follow the way of love, even as Christ loved you. He gave himself for us as an offering to God, a gift of pleasing fragrance.

As for lewd conduct or promiscuousness or lust of any sort, let them not even be mentioned among you; your holiness forbids this. Nor should there be any obscene, silly, or suggestive talk; all that is out of place. Instead, give thanks. Make no mistake about this: no fornicator, no unclean or lustful person—in effect an idolater—has any inheritance in the kingdom of Christ and of God. Let no one deceive you with worthless arguments. These are sins that bring God's wrath down on the disobedient; therefore have nothing to do with them.

There was a time when you were darkness, but now you are light in the Lord. Well, then, live as children of light. Light produces every kind of goodness and justice and truth. Be correct in your judgment of what pleases the Lord. Take no part in vain deeds done in darkness; rather, condemn them. It is shameful even to mention the things these people

E. Service or Neglect of Those in Need:

The description of the last judgment which follows can both reassure our hearts and, at the same time, leave us uneasy. It preaches that God remembers those occasions when we recognized Christ in our needy neighbor and responded accordingly; it also teaches that the Lord recalls those situations when we failed to see Jesus in troubled persons and neglected them.

Unfortunately few, if any of us, can come up with a perfect score on this test. Think of several particularly difficult cases—the confused patient in a nursing home, the emotionally or mentally disturbed, the deeply rebellious youngster, the "con" artist who seeks a handout, the constantly imposing neighbor or relative, the alcoholic, the unpleasant personnel at work—and judge yourself according to the gospel standards.

"When the Son of Man comes in his glory, escorted by all the angels of heaven, he will sit upon his royal throne, and all the nations will be assembled before him. Then he will separate them into two groups, as a shepherd separates sheep from goats. The sheep he will place on his right hand, the goats on his left. The king will say to those on his right: 'Come. You have my Father's blessing! Inherit the kingdom prepared for you from the creation of the world. For I was hungry and you gave me food, I was thirsty and you gave me drink. I was a stranger and you welcomed me, naked and you clothed me. I was ill and you comforted me, in prison and you came to visit me.' Then the just will ask him: 'Lord, when did we see you hungry and feed you or see you thirsty and give you drink? When did we welcome you away from home or clothe you in your nakedness? When did we visit you when you were ill or in prison?' The king will answer them: 'I assure you, as often as you

"Remember to keep holy the sabbath day. Six days you may labor and do all your work, but the seventh day is the sabbath of the LORD, your God. No work may be done then either by you, or your son or daughter, or your male or female slave, or your beast, or by the alien who lives with you. In six days the LORD made the heavens and the earth, the sea and all that is in them; but on the seventh day he rested. That is why the LORD has blessed the sabbath day and made it holy.

"Honor your father and your mother, that you may have a long life in the land which the LORD, your God, is giving you.

"You shall not kill.

"You shall not commit adultery.

"You shall not steal.

"You shall not bear false witness against your neighbor.

"You shall not covet your neighbor's house. You shall not covet your neighbor's wife, nor his male or female slave, nor his ox or ass, nor anything else that belongs to him."

When the people witnessed the thunder and lightning, the trumpet blast and the mountain smoking, they all feared and trembled. So they took up a position much farther away and said to Moses, "You speak to us, and we will listen; but let not God speak to us, or we shall die." Moses answered the people, "Do not be afraid, for God has come to you only to test you and put his fear upon you, lest you should sin." Still the people remained at a distance, while Moses approached the cloud where God was.—
Exodus 20:1-21

LORD said to him. "If anyone kills Cain, Cain shall be avenged sevenfold." So the LORD put a mark on Cain, lest anyone should kill him at sight.
—Genesis 4:1-15

D. The Bare Minimum:

The ten commandments give us good guidelines for our lives. There would be peace on earth, if every person kept these divine rules. Yet the Christian is summoned higher and asked to move beyond those laws.

They form, then, a kind of bare minimum. If we have violated them, we know our lives have slipped below the danger point and certainly cannot call ourselves good Christians. That title is reserved for those who keep these precepts which follow *and* faithfully pursue the course Jesus sketched for us by his life and teaching.

Then God delivered all these commandments:

"I, the LORD, am your God, who brought you out of the land of Egypt, that place of slavery. You shall not have other gods besides me. You shall not carve idols for yourselves in the shape of anything in the sky above or on the earth below or in the waters beneath the earth; you shall not bow down before them or worship them. For I, the LORD, your God, am a jealous God, inflicting punishment for their fathers' wickedness on the children of those who hate me, down to the third and fourth generation; but bestowing mercy down to the thousandth generation, on the children of those who love me and keep my commandments.

"You shall not take the name of the LORD, your God, in vain. For the LORD will not leave unpunished him who takes his name in vain.

shall you get bread to eat,
Until you return to the ground,
    from which you were taken;
For you are dirt,
    and to dirt you shall return."—Genesis 3:1-19

The man had relations with his wife Eve, and she conceived and bore Cain, saying, "I have produced a man with the help of the LORD." Next she bore his brother Abel. Abel became a keeper of flocks, and Cain a tiller of the soil. In the course of time Cain brought an offering to the LORD from the fruit of the soil, while Abel, for his part, brought one of the best firstlings of his flock. The LORD looked with favor on Abel and his offering, but on Cain and his offering he did not. Cain greatly resented this and was crestfallen. So the LORD said to Cain: "Why are you so resentful and crestfallen? If you do well, you can hold up your head; but if not, sin is a demon lurking at the door: his urge is toward you, yet you can be his master."

Cain said to his brother Abel, "Let us go out in the field." When they were in the field, Cain attacked his brother Abel and killed him. Then the LORD asked Cain, "Where is your brother Abel?" He answered, "I do not know. Am I my brother's keeper?" The LORD then said: "What have you done! Listen: your brother's blood cries out to me from the soil! Therefore you shall be banned from the soil that opened its mouth to receive your brother's blood from your hand. If you till the soil, it shall no longer give you its produce. You shall become a restless wanderer on the earth." Cain said to the LORD: "My punishment is too great to bear. Since you have now banished me from the soil, and I must avoid your presence and become a restless wanderer on the earth, anyone may kill me at sight." "Not so!" the

do in secret; but when such deeds are condemned
they are seen in the light of day, and all that then
appears is light. That is why we read:

"Awake, O sleeper,
  arise from the dead,
  and Christ will give you light."

Keep careful watch over your conduct. Do not act
like fools, but like thoughtful men. Make the most of
the present opportunity, for these are evil days. Do
not continue in ignorance, but try to discern the will
of the Lord. Avoid getting drunk on wine; that leads
to debauchery. Be filled with the Spirit, addressing
one another in psalms and hymns and inspired songs.
Sing praise to the Lord with all your hearts. Give
thanks to God the Father always and for everything
in the name of our Lord Jesus Christ.—Ephesians
5:1-20

G. Forgiveness of Others:

If you have been hurt by someone, are nursing a
grudge, just can't forgive, much less forget an offense,
harbor resentment or seek revenge, then God's words
below may say something to you.

Then Peter came up and asked him, "Lord, when
my brother wrongs me, how often must I forgive him?
Seven times?" "No," Jesus replied, "not seven times;
I say, seventy times seven times. That is why the
reign of God may be said to be like a king who
decided to settle accounts with his officials. When
he began his auditing, one was brought in who owed
him a huge amount. As he had no way of paying it,
his master ordered him to be sold, along with his

wife, his children, and all his property, in payment of the debt. At that the official prostrated himself in homage and said, 'My lord, be patient with me and I will pay you back in full.' Moved with pity, the master let the official go and wrote off the debt. But when that same official went out he met a fellow servant who owed him a mere fraction of what he himself owed. He seized him and throttled him. 'Pay back what you owe,' he demanded. His fellow servant dropped to his knees and began to plead with him, 'Just give me time and I will pay you back in full.' But he would hear none of it. Instead, he had him put in jail until he paid back what he owed. When his fellow servants saw what had happened they were badly shaken, and went to their master to report the whole incident. His master sent for him and said, 'You worthless wretch! I canceled your entire debt when you pleaded with me. Should you not have dealt mercifully with your fellow servant, as I dealt with you?" Then in anger the master handed him over to the torturers until he paid back all that he owed. My heavenly Father will treat you in exactly the same way unless each of you forgives his brother from his heart."—Matthew 18:21-35

"You have heard the commandment imposed on your forefathers, 'You shall not commit murder; every murderer shall be liable to judgment.' What I say to you is: everyone who grows angry with his brother shall be liable to judgment; any man who uses abusive language toward his brother shall be answerable to the Sanhedrin, and if he holds him in contempt he risks the fires of Gehenna. If you bring your gift to the altar and there recall that your brother has anything against you, leave your gift at the altar, go first to be reconciled with your brother, and then come and offer your gift. Lose no time; settle with your opponent while on your way to court with him. Otherwise your opponent may hand you over to the guard, who will throw you into prison. I warn you, you will not be released until you have paid the last penny."—Matthew 5:21-26

"You have heard the commandment, 'An eye for an eye, a tooth for a tooth.' But what I say to you is: offer no resistance to injury. When a person strikes you on the right cheek, turn and offer him the other. If anyone wants to go to law over your shirt, hand him your coat as well. Should anyone press you into service for one mile, go with him two miles. Give to the man who begs from you. Do not turn your back on the borrower.

"You have heard the commandment, 'You shall love your countryman but hate your enemy.' My command to you is: love your enemies, pray for your persecutors. This will prove that you are sons of your heavenly Father, for his sun rises on the bad and the good, he rains on the just and the unjust. If you love those who love you, what merit is there in that? Do not tax collectors do as much? And if you greet your brothers only, what is so praiseworthy about that? Do not pagans do as much?"—Matthew 5:38-47

"If you forgive the faults of others, your heavenly Father will forgive you yours. If you do not forgive others, neither will your Father forgive you."—Matthew 6:14-15

There will be no true or deep peace in our hearts until we are willing to forgive those who have injured us.

H. A Call to Prayer:

The bible offers several principles to guide us in our prayer life as Christians.

Pray frequently:

Finally, draw your strength from the Lord and his mighty power. Put on the armor of God so that you may be able to stand firm against the tactics of the devil. Our battle is not against human forces but against the principalities and powers, the rulers of this world of darkness, the evil spirits in regions above. You must put on the armor of God if you are to resist on the evil day; do all that your duty requires, and hold your ground. Stand fast, with the truth as the belt around your waist, justice as your breastplate, and zeal to propagate the gospel of peace as your footgear. In all circumstances hold faith up before you as your shield; it will help you extinguish the fiery darts of the evil one. Take the helmet of salvation and the sword of the spirit, the word of God.

At every opportunity pray in the Spirit, using prayers and petitions of every sort. Pray constantly and attentively for all in the holy company.—Ephesians 6:10-18

Pray from a pure heart for the proper reason:

"Be on guard against performing religious acts for people to see. Otherwise expect no recompense from your heavenly Father. . . . When you are praying, do not behave like the hypocrites who love to stand and pray in synagogues or on street corners in order to be noticed. I give you my word, they are already repaid. Whenever you pray, go to your room, close

your door, and pray to your Father in private. Then
your Father, who sees what no man sees, will repay
you. In your prayer do not rattle on like the pagans.
They think they will win a hearing by the sheer
multiplication of words. Do not imitate them. Your
Father knows what you need before you ask him."
—Matthew 6:1, 5-8

Pray together with others:

"Again I tell you, if two of you join your voices on
earth to pray for anything whatever, it shall be
granted you by my Father in heaven. Where two or
three are gathered in my name, there am I in their
midst."—Matthew 18:19-20

Pray with persistence and confidence:

One day he was praying in a certain place. When
he had finished, one of his disciples asked him, "Lord,
teach us to pray, as John taught his disciples." He
said to them, "When you pray, say:
   "Father,
   hallowed be your name,
   your kingdom come.
   Give us each day our daily bread.
   Forgive us our sins
   for we too forgive all who do us wrong;
   and subject us not to the trial."
Jesus said to them: "If one of you knows someone
who comes to him in the middle of the night and
says to him, 'Friend, lend me three loaves, for a friend
of mine has come in from a journey and I have nothing
to offer him'; and he from inside should reply, 'Leave
me alone. The door is shut now and my children
and I are in bed. I cannot get up to look after your
needs'—I tell you, even though he does not get up

and take care of the man because of friendship, he will do so because of his persistence, and give him as much as he needs.

"So I say to you, 'Ask and you shall receive; seek and you shall find; knock and it shall be opened to you.'

"For whoever asks, receives; whoever seeks, finds; whoever knocks, is admitted. What father among you will give his son a snake if he asks for a fish, or hand him a scorpion if he asks for an egg? If you, with all your sins, know how to give your children good things, how much more will the heavenly Father give the Holy Spirit to those who ask him."
—Luke 11:1-13

How would you evaluate yourself in this area according to these principles?

I. Self-righteously Passing Judgments:

If you really think you are better than someone else, tend to be patronizing, look down on others, quickly judge people or speak unkindly about them, the passages which follow should prove of interest.

"If you want to avoid judgment, stop passing judgment. Your verdict on others will be the verdict passed on you. The measure with which you measure will be used to measure you. Why look at the speck in your brother's eye when you miss the plank in your own? How can you say to your brother, 'Let me take that speck out of your eye,' while all the time the plank remains in your own? You hypocrite! Remove the plank from your own eye first; then you will see clearly to take the speck from your brother's eye."
—Matthew 7:1-5

48

He then spoke this parable addressed to those who believed in their own self-righteousness while holding everyone else in contempt: "Two men went up to the temple to pray; one was a Pharisee, the other a tax collector. The Pharisee with head unbowed prayed in this fashion: 'I give you thanks, O God, that I am not like the rest of men—grasping, crooked, adulterous—or even like this tax collector. I fast twice a week. I pay tithes on all I possess.' The other man, however, kept his distance, not even daring to raise his eyes to heaven. All he did was beat his breast and say, 'O God, be merciful to me, a sinner.' Believe me, this man went home from the temple justified but the other did not. For everyone who exalts himself shall be humbled while he who humbles himself shall be exalted."—Luke 18:9-14

In the name of the encouragement you owe me in Christ, in the name of the solace that love can give, of fellowship in spirit, compassion, and pity, I beg you: make my joy complete by your unanimity, possessing the one love, united in spirit and ideals. Never act out of rivalry or conceit; rather, let all parties think humbly of others as superior to themselves, each of you looking to others' interests rather than to his own.—Philippians 2:1-4

Not many of you should become teachers, my brothers; you should realize that those of us who do so will be called to the stricter account. All of us fall short in many respects. If a person is without fault in speech he is a man in the fullest sense, because he can control his entire body. When we put bits into the mouths of horses to make them obey us, we guide the rest of their bodies. It is the same with ships: however large they are, and despite the fact that they are driven by fierce winds, they are directed

49

by very small rudders on whatever course the steersman's impulse may select. The tongue is something like that. It is a small member, yet it makes great pretensions.

See how tiny the spark is that sets a huge forest ablaze! The tongue is such a flame. It exists among our members as a whole universe of malice. The tongue defiles the entire body. Its flames encircle our course from birth, and its fire is kindled by hell. Every form of life, four-footed or winged, crawling or swimming, can be tamed, and has been tamed, by mankind; the tongue no man can tame. It is a restless evil, full of deadly poison. We use it to say, "Praised be the Lord and Father"; then we use it to curse men, though they are made in the likeness of God. Blessing and curse come out of the same mouth. This ought not to be, my brothers! Does a spring gush forth fresh water and foul from the same outlet? A fig tree, brothers, cannot produce olives, or a grapevine figs; no more can a brackish source yield fresh water.
—James 3:1-12

J. Fidelity in Marriage:

Have you been loyal and true to your partner in good times and in bad, in sickness and in health, when rich and when poor, at 46 as well as 21? There should be no double standard here—a set of strict rules for the wife and a more relaxed code for the husband. Christian teaching demands faithfulness in thought and word, as well as deed.

"You have heard the commandment, 'You shall not commit adultery.' What I say to you is: anyone who looks lustfully at a woman has already committed adultery with her in his thoughts. If your right eye is

your trouble, gouge it out and throw it away! Better
to lose part of your body than to have it all cast into
Gehenna. Again, if your right hand is your trouble
cut it off and throw it away! Better to lose part of
your body than to have it all cast into Gehenna.

It was also said, 'Whenever a man divorces his wife,
he must give her a decree of divorce.' What I say to
you is: everyone who divorces his wife—lewd conduct is a separate case—forces her to commit adultery.
The man who marries a divorced woman likewise
commits adultery."—Matthew 5:27-32

K. Correcting Another:

Few find this a pleasant task. We often run away
from the duty or prefer to withdraw in silence, then
grumble to ourselves or complain to others. Fraternal
correction takes courage, requires pure motives, pre-
supposes sensitivity and does not always succeed. Jesus
urges a few steps in the process.

"If your brother should commit some wrong against
you, go and point out his fault, but keep it between
the two of you. If he listens to you, you have won
your brother over. If he does not listen, summon
another, so that every case may stand on the word of
two or three witnesses. If he ignores them, refer it
to the church. If he ignores even the church, then
treat him as you would a Gentile or a tax collector."
I assure you, whatever you declare bound on earth
shall be held bound in heaven, and whatever you
declare loosed on earth shall be held loosed in heaven.
—Matthew 18:15-18

L. True Riches and Trust in God:

Are you worrying too much and not trusting enough? Overly ambitious? Excessively concerned about money? Unwilling to share what you possess with others?

"Do not lay up for yourselves an earthly treasure. Moths and rust corrode; thieves break in and steal. Make it your practice instead to store up heavenly treasure, which neither moths nor rust corrode nor thieves break in and steal. Remember, where your treasure is, there your heart is also. The eye is the body's lamp. If your eyes are good, your body will be filled with light; if your eyes are bad, your body will be in darkness. And if your light is darkness, how deep will the darkness be! No man can serve two masters. He will either hate one and love the other or be attentive to one and despise the other. You cannot give yourself to God and money. I warn you, then: do not worry about your livelihood, what you are to eat or drink or use for clothing. Is not life more than food? Is not the body more valuable than clothes?

"Look at the birds in the sky. They do not sow or reap, they gather nothing into barns; yet your heavenly Father feeds them. Are not you more important than they? Which of you by worrying can add a moment to his life-span? As for clothes, why be concerned? Learn a lesson from the way the wild flowers grow. They do not work; they do not spin. Yet I assure you, not even Solomon in all his splendor was arrayed like one of these. If God can clothe in such splendor the grass of the field, which blooms today and is thrown on the fire tomorrow, will he not provide much more for you, O weak in faith! Stop worrying, then, over questions like, 'What are we to

eat, or what are we to drink, or what are we to wear?'
The unbelievers are always running after these things.
Your heavenly Father knows all that you need. Seek
first his kingship over you, his way of holiness, and
all these things will be given you besides. Enough,
then, of worrying about tomorrow. Let tomorrow
take care of itself. Today has troubles enough of its
own."—Matthew 6:19-34

M. Guidance from the Church:

In connection with the recently revised Rite of
Penance the Congregation of Divine Worship offered
a suggested outline of questions for use in examining
our consciences.

It first poses three overall inquiries covering certain areas of the past and attitudes about the present.

FORM OF EXAMINATION OF CONSCIENCE*

*In an examination of conscience, before the sacra-
ment of Penance, each individual should ask himself
these questions in particular:*

1. What is my attitude to the sacrament of Penance?
   Do I sincerely want to be set free from sin, to turn
   again to God, to begin a new life, and to enter
   into a deeper friendship with God? Or do I look
   on it as a burden, to be undertaken as seldom as
   possible?

2. Did I forget to mention, or deliberately conceal,
   any grave sins in past confessions?

3. Did I perform the penance I was given? Did I
   make reparation for any injury to others? Have I
   tried to put into practice my resolution to lead a
   better life in keeping with the Gospel?

* © 1975, International Committee on English in the Liturgy.

The "Outline for an Examination of Conscience" then presents the penitent with a lengthy list of questions based on God's words which tell us to love the Lord with our whole heart, to love our neighbor as ourself, and to be perfect as our heavenly Father is perfect.

Each individual should examine his life in the light of God's word.

I.

The Lord says: "You shall love the Lord your God with your whole heart."

1. Is my heart set on God, so that I really love him above all things and am faithful to his commandments, as a son loves his father? Or am I more concerned about the things of this world? Have I a right intention in what I do?

2. God spoke to us in his Son: is my faith in God firm and secure? Am I wholehearted in accepting the Church's teaching? Have I been careful to grow in my understanding of the faith, to hear God's word, to listen to instructions on the faith, to avoid dangers to faith? Have I been always strong and fearless in professing my faith in God and the Church? Have I been willing to be known as a Christian in private and public life?

3. Have I prayed morning and evening? When I pray, do I really raise my mind and heart to God or is it a matter of words only? Do I offer God my difficulties, my joys, and my sorrows? Do I turn to God in time of temptation?

4. Have I love and reverence for God's name? Have I offended him in blasphemy, swearing falsely, or taking his name in vain? Have I shown disrespect for the Blessed Virgin Mary and the saints?

5. Do I keep Sundays and feast days holy by taking a full part, with attention and devotion, in the liturgy, and especially in the Mass? Have I fulfilled the precept of annual confession and of communion during the Easter season?

6. Are there false gods that I worship by giving them greater attention and deeper trust than I give to God: money, superstition, spiritism, or other occult practices?

II.

The Lord says: "Love one another as I have loved you."

1. Have I a genuine love for my neighbor? Or do I use them for my own ends, or do to them what I would not want done to myself? Have I given grave scandal by my words or actions?

2. In my family life, have I contributed to the well-being and happiness of the rest of the family by patience and genuine love? Have I been obedient to parents, showing them proper respect and giving them help in their spiritual and material needs? Have I been careful to give a Christian upbringing to my children, and helped them by good example and by exercising authority as a parent? Have I been faithful to my husband (wife), in my heart and in my relations with others?

55

3. Do I share my possessions with the less fortunate? Do I do my best to help the victims of oppression, misfortune, and poverty? Or do I look down on my neighbor, especially the poor, the sick, the elderly, strangers, and people of other races?

4. Does my life reflect the mission I received in confirmation? Do I share in the apostolic and charitable works of the Church, and in the life of my parish? Have I helped to meet the needs of the Church and of the world, and prayed for them: for unity in the Church, for the spread of the Gospel among the nations, for peace and justice, etc.?

5. Am I concerned for the good and prosperity of the human community in which I live, or do I spend my life caring only for myself? Do I share to the best of my ability in the work of promoting justice, morality, harmony, and love in human relations? Have I done my duty as a citizen? Have I paid my taxes?

6. In my work or profession am I just, hard-working, honest, serving society out of love for others? Have I paid a fair wage to my employees? Have I been faithful to my promises and contracts?

7. Have I obeyed legitimate authority and given it due respect?

8. If I am in a position of responsibility or authority, do I use this for my own advantage or for the good of others, in a spirit of service?

9. Have I been truthful and fair, or have I injured

others by deceit, calumny, detraction, rash judgment, or violation of a secret?

10. Have I done violence to others by damage to life or limb, reputation, honor, or material possessions? Have I involved them in loss? Have I been responsible for advising an abortion or procuring one? Have I kept up hatred for others? Am I estranged from others through quarrels, enmity, insults, anger? Have I been guilty of refusing to testify to the innocence of another because of selfishness?

11. Have I stolen the property of others? Have I desired it unjustly and inordinately? Have I damaged it? Have I made restitution of other people's property and made good their loss?

12. If I have been injured, have I been ready to make peace, for the love of Christ, and to forgive, or do I harbor hatred and the desire for revenge?

III.

Christ our Lord says: "Be perfect as your Father is perfect."

1. Where is my life really leading me? Is the hope of eternal life my inspiration? Have I tried to grow in the life of the Spirit through prayer, reading the word of God and meditating on it, receiving the sacraments, self-denial? Have I been anxious to control my vices, my bad inclinations and passions, e.g., envy, love of food and drink? Have I been proud and boastful, thinking myself better in the sight of God and despising others as less important than myself? Have I imposed my own

will on others, without respecting their freedom and rights?

2. What use have I made of time, of health and strength, of the gifts God has given me to be used like the talents in the Gospel? Do I use them to become more perfect every day? Or have I been lazy and too much given to leisure?

3. Have I been patient in accepting the sorrows and disappointments of life? How have I performed mortification so as to "fill up what is wanting to the sufferings of Christ"? Have I kept the precept of fasting and abstinence?

4. Have I kept my senses and my whole body pure and chaste as a temple of the Holy Spirit consecrated for resurrection and glory, and as a sign of God's faithful love for men and women, a sign that is seen most perfectly in the sacrament of matrimony? Have I dishonored my body by fornication, impurity, unworthy conversation or thoughts, evil desires, or actions? Have I given in to sensuality? Have I indulged in reading, conversation, shows, and entertainments that offend against Christian and human decency? Have I encouraged others to sin by my own failure to maintain these standards? Have I been faithful to the moral law in my married life?

5. Have I gone against my conscience out of fear or hypocrisy?

6. Have I always tried to act in the true freedom of the sons of God according to the law of the Spirit, or am I the slave of forces within me?

Step 4:
The Confession of Sin

The actual confession of sins ideally follows the pattern outlined by the new ritual as indicated below. However, the words you use and the way you say them are of secondary concern. It is the sorrow for sin and the change of heart which really matter.

Should you feel nervous or become forgetful, simply tell the confessor that and ask for his help.

Keep in mind these questions when relating your sins: What did I do? Why did I do it? How can I be better?

At the end of this section you will find two sample confessions which bring out that what, why, how approach.

Some churches provide rooms of reconciliation which offer the opportunity for sit down, face to face confessions as well as for the more customary kneeling behind the screen, anonymous type. When given that choice, simply select the manner you find most comfortable and in which you can confess openly and best find the forgiving peace of Christ.

S
T
E
P
4

Penitents and priests familiar and comfortable with the charismatic view of this sacrament as an occasion for inner healing will find the rite flexible enough to suit that approach. Shared biblical reading, a reflective period seeking the Holy Spirit's guidance, and prayers for healing, deliverance and strengthening can easily be incorporated within its framework.

Regardless of the manner you confess, however, the results should be identical: a sense of forgiveness and freedom, a serenity deep within the heart, a sometimes even conscious awareness of strength received throughout your whole being, a confidence that, reconciled with God, yourself and others, you can move on to a better, happier way of living.

RITE FOR RECONCILIATION
OF INDIVIDUAL PENITENTS[1]

Reception of the Penitent

41. When the penitent comes to confess his sins, the priest welcomes him warmly and greets him with kindness.

42. Then the penitent makes the sign of the cross which the priest may make also.

In the name of the Father, and of the Son, and of the Holy Spirit. Amen.

The priest invites the penitent to have trust in God, in these or similar words:

May God, who has enlightened every heart,
help you to know your sins
and trust in his mercy.

The penitent answers:

Amen.

Or:

The Lord does not wish the sinner to die   [67]
but to turn back to him and live.
Come before him with trust in his mercy.
(Ezechiel 33:11)

---

1. Chapter 1 from the *Rite of Penance*, International Committee on English in the Liturgy, Inc., copyright © 1974, pp. 31-41.

Or:

May the Lord Jesus welcome you.   [68]
He came to call sinners, not the just.
Have confidence in him.   (Luke 5:32)

Or:

May the grace of the Holy Spirit   [69]
fill your heart with light,
that you may confess your sins with loving trust
and come to know that God is merciful.

Or:

May the Lord be in your heart   [70]
and help you to confess your sins with true sorrow.

Or:

If you have sinned, do not lose heart.   [71]
We have Jesus Christ to plead for us with the Father:
he is the holy One,
the atonement for our sins
and for the sins of the whole world.   (1 John 2:1-2)

Reading of the Word of God (optional)

43. Then the priest may read or say from memory a text of Scripture which proclaims God's mercy and calls man to conversion.

> Let us look on Jesus,   [72]
> who suffered to save us
> and rose again for our justification.

Isaiah 53:4-6

**It was our infirmities that he bore,
  our sufferings that he endured,**

While we thought of him as stricken,
  as one smitten by God and afflicted.
But he was pierced for our offenses,
  crushed for our sins;
Upon him was the chastisement that makes us whole,
  by his stripes we were healed.
We had all gone astray like sheep,
  each following his own way;
But the LORD laid upon him the guilt of us all.

Ezechiel 11:19-20   [73]

      Let us listen to the Lord as he speaks to us:

I will give them a new heart and put a new spirit
within them; I will remove the stony heart from their
bodies, and replace it with a natural heart, so that
they will live according to my statutes, and observe
and carry out my ordinances; thus they shall be my
people and I will be their God.

Matthew 6:14-15   [74]

      Let us listen to the Lord as he speaks to us:

"If you forgive the faults of others, your heavenly
Father will forgive you yours. If you do not forgive
others, neither will your Father forgive you."

Mark 1:14-15   [75]

After John's arrest, Jesus appeared in Galilee
proclaiming the good news of God: "This is the time
of fulfillment. The reign of God is at hand! Reform
your lives and believe in the gospel!"

63

Do to others what you would have them do to you.
If you love those who love you, what credit is that to
you? Even sinners love those who love them. If you
do good to those who do good to you, how can you
claim any credit? Sinners do as much. If you lend to
those from whom you expect repayment, what merit is
there in it for you? Even sinners lend to sinners,
expecting to be repaid in full.

"Love your enemy and do good; lend without
expecting repayment. Then will your recompense be
great. You will rightly be called sons of the Most
High, since he himself is good to the ungrateful and
the wicked.

"Be compassionate, as your Father is
compassionate. Do not judge, and you will not be
judged. Do not condemn, and you will not be
condemned. Pardon, and you shall be pardoned.
Give, and it shall be given to you. Good measure
pressed down, shaken together, running over, will they
pour into the fold of your garment. For the measure
you measure with will be measured back to you."

The tax collectors and sinners were all gathering
around to hear him, at which the Pharisees and the
scribes murmured, "This man welcomes sinners and
eats with them." Then he addressed this parable to
them: "Who among you, if he has a hundred sheep and
loses one of them, does not leave the ninety-nine in
the wasteland and follow the lost one until he finds
it? And when he finds it, he puts it on his shoulders in
jubilation. Once arrived home, he invites friends and
neighbors in and says to them, 'Rejoice with me

because I have found my lost sheep.' I tell you, there
will likewise be more joy in heaven over one repentant
sinner than over ninety-nine righteous people who
have no need to repent."

John 20:19-23 [78]

On the evening of that first day of the week, even
though the disciples had locked the doors of the place
where they were for fear of the Jews, Jesus came and
stood before them. "Peace be with you," he said.
When he had said this, he showed them his hands and
his side. At the sight of the Lord the disciples rejoiced.
"Peace be with you," he said again.

"As the Father has sent me,
so I send you."

Then he breathed on them and said:

"Receive the Holy Spirit.
If you forgive men's sins,
they are forgiven them;
if you hold them bound,
they are held bound."

Romans 5:8-9 [79]

It is precisely in this that God proves his love for us:
that while we were still sinners, Christ died for us.
Now that we have been justified by his blood, it is all
the more certain that we shall be saved by him from
God's wrath.

Ephesians 5:1-2 [80]

Be imitators of God as his dear children. Follow the

way of love, even as Christ loved you. He gave himself for us as an offering to God, a gift of pleasing fragrance.

Colossians 1:12-14   [81]

Give thanks to the Father for having made you worthy to share the lot of the saints in light.
He rescued us from the power of darkness and brought us into the kingdom of his beloved Son.
Through him we have redemption, the forgiveness of our sins.

Colossians 3:8-10, 12-17   [82]

You must put that aside now: all the anger and quick temper, the malice, the insults, the foul language. Stop lying to one another. What you have done is put aside your old self with its past deeds and put on a new man, one who grows in knowledge as he is formed anew in the image of his Creator. Because you are God's chosen ones, holy and beloved, clothe yourselves with heartfelt mercy, with kindness, humility, meekness, and patience. Bear with one another; forgive whatever grievances you have against one another. Forgive as the Lord has forgiven you. Over all these virtues put on love, which binds the rest together and makes them perfect. Christ's peace must reign in your hearts, since as members of the one body you have been called to that peace. Dedicate yourselves to thankfulness. Let the word of Christ, rich as it is, dwell in you. In wisdom made perfect, instruct and admonish one another. Sing gratefully to God from your hearts in psalms, hymns, and inspired songs. Whatever you do, whether in speech or in action, do it in the name of the Lord Jesus. Give thanks to God the Father through him.

If we say, "We have fellowship with him,"
while continuing to walk in darkness,
we are liars and do not act in truth.
But if we walk in light,
as he is in the light,
we have fellowship with one another,
and the blood of his Son Jesus cleanses us from all sin.
But if we acknowledge our sins,
he who is just can be trusted
to forgive our sins
and cleanse us from every wrong.

[84]

A reading may also be chosen from those given in nos. 101-201 for the reconciliation of several penitents. The priest and penitent may choose other readings from scripture.

Confession of Sins and Acceptance of Satisfaction

44. Where it is the custom, the penitent says a general formula for confession (for example, I confess to almighty God) before he confesses his sins.

If necessary, the priest helps the penitent to make an integral confession and gives him suitable counsel. He urges him to be sorry for his faults, reminding him that through the sacrament of penance the Christian dies and rises with Christ and is thus renewed in the paschal mystery. The priest proposes an act of penance which the penitent accepts to make satisfaction for sin and to amend his life.

The priest should make sure that he adapts his counsel to the penitent's circumstances.

Prayer of the Penitent and Absolution

45. The priest then asks the penitent to express his sorrow, which the penitent may do in these or similar words:

My God,
I am sorry for my sins with all my heart.
In choosing to do wrong
and failing to do good,
I have sinned against you
whom I should love above all things.
I firmly intend, with your help,
to do penance,
to sin no more,
and to avoid whatever leads me to sin.
Our Savior Jesus Christ
suffered and died for us.
In his name, my God, have mercy.

Or:

Remember, O Lord, your compassion and [85]
    mercy which you showed long ago.
Do not recall the sins and failings of my youth.
In your mercy remember me, Lord, because of your
    goodness. (Psalm 25:6-7)

Or:

Wash me from my guilt [86]
and cleanse me of my sin.
I acknowledge my offense;
my sin is before me always. (Ps 51:4-5)

Or:

Father, I have sinned against you [87]
and am not worthy to be called your son.
Be merciful to me, a sinner. (Luke 15:18; 18:13)

Or:

Father of mercy,   [88]
like the prodigal son
I return to you and say:
"I have sinned against you
and am no longer worthy to be called your son."
Christ Jesus, Savior of the world,
I pray with the repentant thief
to whom you promised Paradise:
"Lord, remember me in your kingdom."
Holy Spirit, fountain of love,
I call on you with trust:
"Purify my heart,
and help me to walk as a child of light."

Or:

Lord Jesus,   [89]
you opened the eyes of the blind,
healed the sick,
forgave the sinful woman,
and after Peter's denial confirmed him in your love.
Listen to my prayer:
forgive all my sins,
renew your love in my heart,
help me to live in perfect unity with my fellow
      Christians
that I may proclaim your saving power to all the world.

Or:

Lord Jesus,   [90]
you chose to be called the friend of sinners.
By your saving death and resurrection
free me from my sins.
May your peace take root in my heart
and bring forth a harvest
of love, holiness, and truth.

Or:

Lord Jesus Christ,   [91]
you are the Lamb of God;
you take away the sins of the world.
Through the grace of the Holy Spirit
restore me to friendship with your Father,
cleanse me from every stain of sin
in the blood you shed for me,
and raise me to new life
for the glory of your name.

Or:

Lord God,   [92]
in your goodness have mercy on me:
do not look on my sins,
but take away all my guilt.
Create in me a clean heart
and renew within me an upright spirit.

Or:

Lord Jesus, Son of God,
have mercy on me, a sinner.

46. Then the priest extends his hands over the penitent's head (or at least extends his right hand) and says:

God, the Father of mercies,
through the death and resurrection of his Son
has reconciled the world to himself
and sent the Holy Spirit among us
for the forgiveness of sins;
through the ministry of the Church
may God give you pardon and peace,
and I absolve you from your sins
in the name of the Father, and of the Son,+
and of the Holy Spirit.

The penitent answers:

Amen.

Proclamation of Praise of God and Dismissal

47. After the absolution, the priest continues:

Give thanks to the Lord, for he is good.

> *The penitent concludes:*

His mercy endures for ever.

> *Then the priest dismisses the penitent who has been reconciled, saying:*

The Lord has freed you from your sins. Go in peace.

Or: [93]

May the Passion of our Lord Jesus Christ,
the intercession of the Blessed Virgin Mary
    and of all the saints,
whatever good you do and suffering you endure,
heal your sins,
help you to grow in holiness,
and reward you with eternal life.
Go in peace.

Or:

The Lord has freed you from sin.
May he bring you safely to his kingdom in heaven.
Glory to him for ever.

Amen.

Or:

Blessed are those
whose sins have been forgiven,
whose evil deeds have been forgotten.
Rejoice in the Lord,
and go in peace.

71

Or:

Go in peace,
and proclaim to the world
the wonderful works of God,
who has brought you salvation.

Some Sample Confessions of Sin

A. "Forgive me, Father. I'm a married man. It's been a month since my last confession. I got angry and lost my temper at the children. This happens often now when I get home from work. I'm tired and I don't want to be bothered.

"I know this is selfish. My anger just makes things worse. I'll try to spend more time with the kids and listen to them instead of yell. Where should I start? Have you any advice?"[2]

B. "Help me, Father, to make a good confession. I'm a fourth grade girl and it has been three months since my last confession.

"I have a brother in the second grade and we are always getting into fights and then my mom and dad get mad at us. I think I fight with him so much because I feel he's my dad's favorite and I'm jealous of him. I'm going to try to think more about the attention that dad gives to me and forget about noticing all the attention that my brother gets.

"I am sorry for this sin and will try to change my attitude toward my brother."

---

2. Sample confession in *I Confess* by Francis J. Buckley, S.J., Ave Maria Press, Notre Dame, Indiana, 1972, pp. 86-87.

Step 5:
Penances for the Past and for the Future

The confessor imposes upon you a penance or satisfaction for your sins as the final step in this sacrament of reconciliation. Designed to repair the harm done and to heal the wounds caused by these misdeeds, it is also intended to help you improve in the days ahead. He will, as your penance, assign a prayer or prayers, propose some action related to a particular sin confessed, or designate one, perhaps several of the readings below. The priest may even offer to read with you the biblical passage selected before pronouncing the words of absolution and forgiveness.

1. Happiness of the Forgiven Sinner

PSALM 32

I

Happy is he whose fault is taken away,
  whose sin is covered.
Happy the man to whom the LORD imputes not guilt,
  in whose spirit there is no guile.

II

As long as I would not speak, my bones wasted away
  with my groaning all the day,
For day and night your hand was heavy upon me;

73

my strength was dried up as by the heat of summer.
Then I acknowledged my sin to you,
   my guilt I covered not.
I said, "I confess my faults to the LORD,"
   and you took away the guilt of my sin.
For this shall every faithful man pray to you
   in time of stress.
Though deep waters overflow,
   they shall not reach him.
You are my shelter; from distress you will preserve me;
   with glad cries of freedom you will ring me round.

III

I will instruct you and show you the way you should
    walk;
   I will counsel you, keeping my eye on you.
Be not senseless like horses or mules:
   with bit and bridle their temper must be curbed,
   else they will not come near you.

IV

Many are the sorrows of the wicked,
   but kindness surrounds him who trusts in the LORD.
Be glad in the LORD and rejoice, you just;
   exult, all you upright of heart.

2. The Miserere: A Prayer of Repentance

PSALM 51

A

Have mercy on me, O God, in your goodness;
   in the greatness of your compassion wipe out my
    offense.

Thoroughly wash me from my guilt
  and of my sin cleanse me.

B

I

For I acknowledge my offense,
  and my sin is before me always;
"Against you only have I sinned,
  and done what is evil in your sight"—
That you may be justified in your sentence,
  vindicated when you condemn.
Indeed, in guilt was I born,
  and in sin my mother conceived me;
Behold, you are pleased with sincerity of heart,
  and in my inmost being you teach me wisdom.

II

Cleanse me of sin with hyssop, that I may be purified;
  wash me, and I shall be whiter than snow.
Let me hear the sounds of joy and gladness;
  the bones you have crushed shall rejoice.
Turn away your face from my sins,
  and blot out all my guilt.

III

A clean heart create for me, O God,
  and a steadfast spirit renew within me.
Cast me not out from your presence,
  and your holy spirit take not from me.
Give me back the joy of your salvation,
  and a willing spirit sustain in me.

I will teach transgressors your ways,
and sinners shall return to you.
Free me from blood guilt, O God, my saving God;
then my tongue shall revel in your justice.
O Lord, open my lips,
and my mouth shall proclaim your praise.
For you are not pleased with sacrifices;
should I offer a holocaust, you would not accept it.
My sacrifice, O God, is a contrite spirit;
a heart contrite and humbled, O God, you will not
spurn.

C

Be bountiful, O LORD, to Zion in your kindness
by rebuilding the walls of Jerusalem;
Then shall you be pleased with due sacrifices,
burnt offerings and holocausts;
then shall they offer up bullocks on your altar.

3. A Distressed Sinner's Prayer for Help

PSALM 143

I

O LORD, hear my prayer;
hearken to my pleading in your faithfulness;
in your justice answer me.
And enter not into judgment with your servant,
for before you no living man is just.

For the enemy pursues me;
  he has crushed my life to the ground;
  he has left me dwelling in the dark, like those long
    dead.
And my spirit is faint within me,
  my heart within me is appalled.
I remember the days of old;
  I meditate on all your doings,
  the works of your hands I ponder.
I stretch out my hands to you;
  my soul thirsts for you like parched land.

III

Hasten to answer me, O LORD, for my spirit fails me.
Hide not your face from me
  lest I become like those who go down into the pit.
At dawn let me hear of your kindness,
  for in you I trust.
Show me the way in which I should walk,
  for to you I lift up my soul.
Rescue me from my enemies, O LORD,
  for in you I hope.

4. The Beatitudes in Luke

Coming down the mountain with them, he stopped
at a level stretch where there were many of his
disciples; a large crowd of people was with them from
all Judea and Jerusalem and the coast of Tyre and Sidon,
people who came to hear him and be healed of their
diseases. Those who were troubled with unclean
spirits were cured; indeed, the whole crowd was
trying to touch him because power went out from him
which cured all. Then, raising his eyes to his disciples,
he said:

"Blest are you poor; the reign of God is yours.
Blest are you who hunger; you shall be filled.
Blest are you who are weeping; you shall laugh.
"Blest shall you be when men hate you, when they
ostracize you and insult you and proscribe your
name as evil because of the Son of Man. On the
day they do so, rejoice and exult, for your reward
shall be great in heaven. Thus it was that their fathers
treated the prophets.

"But woe to you rich, for your consolation is now.
Woe to you who are full; you shall go hungry.
Woe to you who laugh now; you shall weep in your
    grief.

"Woe to you when all speak well of you. Their fathers
treated the false prophets in just this way."
—Luke 6:17-26

The Beatitudes in Matthew

When he saw the crowds he went up on the
mountainside. After he had sat down his disciples
gathered around him, and he began to teach them:

"How blest are the poor in spirit:
    the reign of God is theirs.
Blest too are the sorrowing; they shall be consoled.
[Blest are the lowly; they shall inherit the land.]
Blest are they who hunger and thirst for holiness;
they shall have their fill.
Blest are they who show mercy; mercy shall be theirs.
Blest are the single-hearted for they shall see God.
Blest too the peacemakers; they shall be called sons of
    God.
Blest are those persecuted for holiness' sake; the reign
    of God is theirs.
Blest are you when they insult you and persecute you

78

and utter every kind of slander against you because
of me.
Be glad and rejoice, for your reward is great in
     heaven;
they persecuted the prophets before you in the
     very same way."—Matthew 5:1-12

5. Jesus' Teaching About the Cross

Jesus then said to his disciples: "If a man wishes to
come after me, he must deny his very self, take up his
cross, and begin to follow in my footsteps. Whoever
would save his life will lose it, but whoever loses his life
for my sake will find it. What profit would a man
show if he were to gain the whole world and destroy
himself in the process? What can a man offer in
exchange for his very self? The Son of Man will come
with his Father's glory accompanied by his angels.
When he does, he will repay each man according to
his conduct. I assure you, among those standing here
there are some who will not experience death before
they see the Son of Man come in his kingship."
—Matthew 16:24-28

6. The Need for Watchfulness

"The coming of the Son of Man will repeat what
happened in Noah's time. In the days before the flood
people were eating and drinking, marrying and being
married, right up to the day Noah entered the ark.
They were totally unconcerned until the flood came
and destroyed them. So will it be at the coming of the
Son of Man. Two men will be out in the field; one will
be taken and one will be left. Two women will be
grinding meal; one will be taken and one will be left.
Stay awake, therefore! You cannot know the day your
Lord is coming.

"Be sure of this: if the owner of the house knew when the thief was coming he would keep a watchful eye and not allow his house to be broken into. You must be prepared in the same way. The Son of Man is coming at the time you least expect. Who is the faithful, farsighted servant whom the master has put in charge of his household to dispense food at need? Happy that servant whom his master discovers at work on his return! I assure you, he will put him in charge of all his property. But if the servant is worthless and tells himself, 'My master is a long time in coming,' and begins to beat his fellow servants, to eat and drink with drunkards, that man's master will return when he is not ready and least expects him. He will punish him severely and settle with him as is done with hypocrites. There will be wailing then and grinding of teeth."—Matthew 24:37-51

7. Love for Others, Especially Our Enemies

"To you who hear me, I say: Love your enemies, do good to those who hate you; bless those who curse you and pray for those who maltreat you. When someone slaps you on one cheek, turn and give him the other; when someone takes your coat, let him have your shirt as well. Give to all who beg from you. When a man takes what is yours, do not demand it back. Do to others what you would have them do to you. If you love those who love you, what credit is that to you? Even sinners love those who love them. If you do good to those who do good to you, how can you claim any credit? Sinners do as much. If you lend to those from whom you expect repayment, what merit is there in it for you? Even sinners lend to sinners, expecting to be repaid in full.

"Love your enemy and do good; lend without expecting repayment. Then will your recompense be great. You will rightly be called sons of the Most High, since he himself is good to the ungrateful and the wicked.

"Be compassionate, as your Father is compassionate. Do not judge, and you will not be judged. Do not condemn, and you will not be condemned. Pardon, and you shall be pardoned. Give, and it shall be given to you. Good measure pressed down, shaken together, running over, will they pour into the fold of your garment. For the measure you measure with will be measured back to you."
—Luke 6:27-38

8. Christ's Promise of Peace

"I will not leave you orphaned;
I will come back to you.
A little while now and the world will see me no more;
but you see me
as one who has life, and you will have life.
On that day you will know
that I am in my Father,
and you in me, and I in you.
He who obeys the commandments he has from me
is the man who loves me;
and he who loves me will be loved by my Father.
I too will love him
and reveal myself to him."

Judas (not Judas Iscariot) said to him, "Lord, why is it that you will reveal yourself to us and not to the world?" Jesus answered:

"Anyone who loves me
will be true to my word,
and my Father will love him;
we will come to him

81

and make our dwelling place with him.
He who does not love me does not keep my words.
Yet the word you hear is not mine;
it comes from the Father who sent me.
This much have I told you while I was still with you;
the Paraclete, the Holy Spirit
whom the Father will send in my name,
will instruct you in everything,
and remind you of all that I told you.
'Peace' is my farewell to you,
my peace is my gift to you;
I do not give it to you as the world gives peace.
Do not be distressed or fearful.
You have heard me say,
'I go away for a while, and I come back to you.'
If you truly loved me
you would rejoice to have me go to the Father,
for the Father is greater than I.
I tell you this now, before it takes place,
so that when it takes place you may believe.
I shall not go on speaking to you longer;
the Prince of this world is at hand.
He has no hold on me,
but the world must know that I love the Father
and do as the Father has commanded me.
Come, then! Let us be on our way."—John 14:18-31

9. The Vine and the Branches

"I am the true vine
and my Father is the vinegrower.
He prunes away
every barren branch,
but the fruitful ones
he trims clean
to increase their yield.
You are clean already,

thanks to the word I have spoken to you.
Live on in me, as I do in you.
No more than a branch can bear fruit of itself
apart from the vine,
can you bear fruit
apart from me.
I am the vine, you are the branches.
He who lives in me and I in him,
will produce abundantly,
for apart from me you can do nothing.
A man who does not live in me
is like a withered, rejected branch,
picked up to be thrown in the fire and burnt.
If you live in me,
and my words stay part of you,
you may ask what you will—
it will be done for you.
My Father has been glorified
in your bearing much fruit
and becoming my disciples."—John 15:1-8

10. The Lord's Command to Love

"As the Father has loved me,
so I have loved you.
Live on in my love.
You will live in my love
if you keep my commandments,
even as I have kept my Father's commandments,
and live in his love.
All this I tell you
that my joy may be yours
and your joy may be complete.
This is my commandment:
love one another
as I have loved you.
There is no greater love than this:

to lay down one's life for one's friends.
You are my friends
if you do what I command you.
I no longer speak of you as slaves,
for a slave does not know what his master is about.
Instead, I call you friends,
since I have made known to you all that I heard from
  my Father.
It was not you who chose me,
it was I who chose you
to go forth and bear fruit.
Your fruit must endure,
so that all you ask the Father in my name
he will give you.
The command I give you is this,
that you love one another."—John 15:9-17

11. Dead to Sin, Alive in God

What, then, are we to say? "Let us continue in sin that
grace may abound"? Certainly not! How can we who
died to sin go on living in it? Are you not aware that
we who were baptized into Christ Jesus were baptized
into his death? Through baptism into his death we
were buried with him, so that, just as Christ was raised
from the dead by the glory of the Father, we too
might live a new life. If we have been united with him
through likeness to his death, so shall we be through
a like resurrection. This we know: our old self was
crucified with him so that the sinful body might be
destroyed and we might be slaves to sin no longer. A
man who is dead has been freed from sin. If we have
died with Christ, we believe that we are also to live
with him. We know that Christ, once raised from the
dead, will never die again; death has no more power
over him. His death was death to sin, once for all;
his life is life for God. In the same way, you must

consider yourselves dead to sin but alive for God in Christ Jesus.

Do not, therefore, let sin rule your mortal body and make you obey its lusts; no more shall you offer the members of your body to sin as weapons for evil. Rather, offer yourselves to God as men who have come back from the dead to life, and your bodies to God as weapons for justice. Sin will no longer have power over you; you are now under grace, not under the law.—Romans 6:1-14

12. Freed from Sin, Slaves for God

What does all this lead to? Just because we are not under the law but under grace, are we free to sin? By no means! You must realize that, when you offer yourselves to someone as obedient slaves, you are the slaves of the one you obey, whether yours is the slavery of sin, which leads to death, or of obedience, which leads to justice. Thanks be to God, though once you were slaves of sin, you sincerely obeyed that rule of teaching which was imparted to you; freed from your sin, you became slaves of justice. (I use the following example from human affairs because of your weak human nature.) Just as formerly you enslaved your bodies to impurity and licentiousness for their degradation, make them now the servants of justice for their sanctification. When you were slaves of sin, you had freedom from justice. What benefit did you then enjoy? Things you are now ashamed of, all of them tending toward death. But now that you are freed from sin and have become slaves of God, your benefit is sanctification as you tend toward eternal life. The wages of sin is death, but the gift of God is eternal life in Christ Jesus our Lord.
—Romans 6:15-23

13. Conflict Within Us Between Good and Evil

We know that the law is spiritual, whereas I am weak flesh sold into the slavery of sin. I cannot even understand my own actions. I do not do what I want to do but what I hate. When I act against my own will, by that very fact I agree that the law is good. This indicates that it is not I who do it but sin which resides in me. I know that no good dwells in me, that is, in my flesh; the desire to do right is there but not the power. What happens is that I do, not the good I will to do, but the evil I do not intend. But if I do what is against my will, it is not I who do it, but sin which dwells in me. This means that even though I want to do what is right, a law that leads to wrong-doing is always ready at hand. My inner self agrees with the law of God, but I see in my body's members another law at war with the law of my mind; this makes me the prisoner of the law of sin in my members. What a wretched man I am! Who can free me from this body under the power of death? All praise to God, through Jesus Christ our Lord! So with my mind I serve the law of God but with my flesh the law of sin.—Romans 7:14-25

14. God's Help for Our Weakness

The Spirit too helps us in our weakness, for we do not know how to pray as we ought; but the Spirit himself makes intercession for us with groanings that cannot be expressed in speech. He who searches hearts knows what the Spirit means, for the Spirit intercedes for the saints as God himself wills.

We know that God makes all things work together for the good of those who have been called according to his decree. Those whom he foreknew he predestined to share the image of his Son, that the

Son might be the first-born of many brothers. Those he predestined he likewise called; those he called he also justified; and those he justified he in turn glorified. What shall we say after that? If God is for us, who can be against us? Is it possible that he who did not spare his own Son but handed him over for the sake of us all will not grant us all things besides?
—Romans 8:26-32

15. Clinging to Christ in the Midst of Difficulties

What shall we say after that? If God is for us, who can be against us? Is it possible that he who did not spare his own Son but handed him over for the sake of us all will not grant us all things besides? Who shall bring a charge against God's chosen ones? God, who justifies? Who shall condemn them? Christ Jesus, who died or rather was raised up, who is at the right hand of God and who intercedes for us? Who will separate us from the love of Christ? Trial, or distress, or persecution, or hunger, or nakedness, or danger, or the sword? As Scripture says: "For your sake we are being slain all the day long; we are looked upon as sheep to be slaughtered." Yet in all this we are more than conquerors because of him who has loved us. For I am certain that neither death nor life, neither angels nor principalities, neither the present nor the future, nor powers, neither height nor depth nor any other creature, will be able to separate us from the love of God that comes to us in Christ Jesus, our Lord.—Romans 8:31-39

16. A Call to Love Others

And now, brothers, I beg you through the mercy of God to offer your bodies as a living sacrifice holy and acceptable to God, your spiritual worship. Do not conform yourselves to this age but be transformed by the renewal of your mind, so that you may judge what is God's will, what is good, pleasing and perfect.

Your love must be sincere. Detest what is evil, cling to what is good. Love one another with the affection of brothers. Anticipate each other in showing respect. Do not grow slack but be fervent in spirit; he whom you serve is the Lord. Rejoice in hope, be patient under trial, persevere in prayer. Look on the needs of the saints as your own; be generous in offering hospitality. Bless your persecutors; bless and do not curse them. Rejoice with those who rejoice, weep with those who weep. Have the same attitude toward all. Put away ambitious thoughts and associate with those who are lowly. Do not be wise in your own estimation. Never repay injury with injury. See that your conduct is honorable in the eyes of all. If possible, live peaceably with everyone. Beloved, do not avenge yourselves; leave that to God's wrath, for it is written: " 'Vengeance is mine; I will repay,' says the Lord." But "if your enemy is hungry, feed him; if he is thirsty, give him something to drink; by doing this you will heap burning coals upon his head." Do not be conquered by evil but conquer evil with good.—Romans 12:1-2, 9-21

17. Our Salvation Is Due to God's Loving Mercy

You were dead because of your sins and offenses, as you gave allegiance to the present age and to the prince of the air, that spirit who is even now at work among the rebellious. All of us were once of their company; we lived at the level of the flesh, following every whim and fancy, and so by nature deserved God's wrath like the rest. But God is rich in mercy; because of his great love for us he brought us to life with Christ when we were dead in sin. By this favor

88

you were saved. Both with and in Christ Jesus he raised us up and gave us a place in the heavens, that in the ages to come he might display the great wealth of his favor, manifested by his kindness to us in Christ Jesus. I repeat, it is owing to his favor that salvation is yours through faith. This is not your own doing, it is God's gift; neither is it a reward for anything you have accomplished, so let no one pride himself on it. We are truly his handiwork, created in Christ Jesus to lead the life of good deeds which God prepared for us in advance.—Ephesians 2:1-10

18. An Exhortation to Live in Christian Unity

I plead with you, then, as a prisoner for the Lord, to live a life worthy of the calling you have received, with perfect humility, meekness, and patience, bearing with one another lovingly. Make every effort to preserve the unity which has the Spirit as its origin and peace as its binding force. There is but one body and one Spirit, just as there is but one hope given all of you by your call. There is one Lord, one faith, one baptism; one God and Father of all, who is over all, and works through all, and is in all.
Each of us has received God's favor in the measure in which Christ bestows it.—Ephesians 4:1-7

19. Some Vices To Be Avoided

I declare and solemnly attest in the Lord that you must no longer live as the pagans do—their minds empty, their understanding darkened. They are estranged from a life in God because of their ignorance and their resistance; without remorse they have abandoned themselves to lust and the indulgence of every sort of lewd conduct. That is not what you learned when you learned Christ! I am supposing, of course, that he has been preached and taught to you in accord with the truth that is in Jesus: namely, that you must lay aside your former way of life and old self which deteriorates through illusion and desire, and acquire a fresh, spiritual way of thinking. You must put on that new man created in God's image, whose justice and holiness are born of truth.

See to it, then, that you put an end to lying; let everyone speak the truth to his neighbor, for we are members of one another. If you are angry, let it be without sin. The sun must not go down on your wrath; do not give the devil a chance to work on you. The man who has been stealing must steal no longer; rather, let him work with his hands at honest labor so that he will have something to share with those in need. Never let evil talk pass your lips; say only the good things men need to hear, things that will really help them. Do nothing to sadden the Holy Spirit with whom you were sealed against the day of redemption. Get rid of all bitterness, all passion and anger, harsh words, slander, and malice of every kind. In place of these, be kind to one another, compassionate, and mutually forgiving, just as God has forgiven you in Christ.—Ephesians 4:17-32

20. The Christian's Need for Continued Progress

Ever since we heard this we have been praying for you unceasingly and asking that you may attain full knowledge of his will through perfect wisdom and spiritual insight. Then you will lead a life worthy of the Lord and pleasing to him in every way. You will multiply good works of every sort and grow in the knowledge of God. By the might of his glory you will be endowed with the strength needed to stand fast, even to endure joyfully whatever may come, giving thanks to the Father for having made you worthy to

share the lot of the saints in light. He rescued us from the power of darkness and brought us into the kingdom of his beloved Son. Through him we have redemption, the forgiveness of our sins.
—Colossians 1:9-14

21. Casting Aside the Old Self and Putting on the New Man in Christ

Since you have been raised up in company with Christ, set your heart on what pertains to higher realms where Christ is seated at God's right hand. Be intent on things above rather than on things of earth. After all, you have died! Your life is hidden now with Christ in God. When Christ our life appears, then you shall appear with him in glory.

Put to death whatever in your nature is rooted in earth: fornication, uncleanness, passion, evil desires, and that lust which is idolatry. These are the sins which provoke God's wrath. Your own conduct was once of this sort, when these sins were your very life. You must put that aside now: all the anger and quick temper, the malice, the insults, the foul language. Stop lying to one another. What you have done is put aside your old self with its past deeds and put on a new man, one who grows in knowledge as he is formed anew in the image of his Creator. There is no Greek or Jew here, circumcised or uncircumcised, foreigner, Scythian, slave, or freeman. Rather, Christ is everything in all of you.

Because you are God's chosen ones, holy and beloved, clothe yourselves with heartfelt mercy, with kindness, humility, meekness, and patience. Bear with one another; forgive whatever grievances you have against one another. Forgive as the Lord has forgiven you. Over all these virtues put on love, which binds the rest together and makes them perfect. Christ's peace

must reign in your hearts, since as members of the one body you have been called to that peace. Dedicate yourselves to thankfulness. Let the word of Christ, rich as it is, dwell in you. In wisdom made perfect, instruct and admonish one another. Sing gratefully to God from your hearts in psalms, hymns, and inspired songs. Whatever you do, whether in speech or in action, do it in the name of the Lord Jesus. Give thanks to God the Father through him.
—Colossians 3:1-17

22. God Calls Us to Holiness, Not Immorality

Now, my brothers, we beg and exhort you in the Lord Jesus that even as you learned from us how to conduct yourselves in a way pleasing to God—which you are indeed doing—so you must learn to make still greater progress. You know the instructions we gave you in the Lord Jesus. It is God's will that you grow in holiness: that you abstain from immorality, each of you guarding his member in sanctity and honor, not in passionate desire as do the Gentiles who know not God; and that each refrain from over-reaching or cheating his brother in the matter at hand; for the Lord is an avenger of all such things, as we once indicated to you by our testimony. God has not called us to immorality but to holiness, hence, whoever rejects these instructions rejects, not man, but God who sends his Holy Spirit upon you.

As regards brotherly love, there is no need for me to write you. God himself has taught you to love one another, and this you are doing with respect to all the brothers throughout Macedonia. Yet we exhort you to even greater progress, brothers. Make it a point of honor to remain at peace and attend to your own affairs. Work with your hands as we directed you to do, so that you will give good example to outsiders and want for nothing.—1 Thessalonians 4:1-12

23. Hearing the Lord's Word and Acting on It

Humbly welcome the word that has taken root in you, with its power to save you. Act on this word. If all you do is listen to it, you are deceiving yourselves.

A man who listens to God's word but does not put it into practice is like a man who looks into a mirror at the face he was born with; he looks at himself, then goes off and promptly forgets what he looked like. There is, on the other hand, the man who peers into freedom's ideal law and abides by it. He is no forgetful listener, but one who carries out the law in practice. Blest will this man be in whatever he does.

If a man who does not control his tongue imagines that he is devout, he is self-deceived; his worship is pointless. Looking after orphans and widows in their distress and keeping oneself unspotted by the world make for pure worship without stain before our God and Father.—James 1:21-27

24. Faith and Good Works

My brothers, what good is it to profess faith without practicing it? Such faith has no power to save one, has it? If a brother or sister has nothing to wear and no food for the day, and you say to them, "Goodbye and good luck! Keep warm and well fed," but do not meet their bodily needs, what good is that? So it is with the faith that does nothing in practice. It is thoroughly lifeless.

To such a person one might say, "You have faith and I have works—is that it?" Show me your faith without works, and I will show you the faith that underlies my works! Do you believe that God is one? You are quite right. The demons believe that, and shudder. Do you want proof, you ignoramus, that without works faith is idle? Was not our father

Abraham justified by his works when he offered his son Isaac on the altar? There you see proof that faith was both assisting his works and implemented by his works. You also see how the Scripture was fulfilled which says, "Abraham believed God, and it was credited to him as justice"; for this he received the title "God's friend."

You must perceive that a person is justified by his works and not by faith alone. Rahab the harlot will illustrate the point. Was she not justified by her works when she harbored the messengers and sent them out by a different route? Be assured, then, that faith without works is as dead as a body without breath.
—James 2:14-26

25. Command to Love in Deed and Truth

See what love the Father has bestowed on us
in letting us be called children of God!
Yet that is what we are.
The reason the world does not recognize us
is that it never recognized the Son.
Dearly beloved,
we are God's children now;
what we shall later be has not yet come to light.
We know that when it comes to light
we shall be like him,
for we shall see him as he is.
Everyone who has this hope based on him
keeps himself pure, as he is pure.

Everyone who sins acts lawlessly,
for sin is lawlessness.
You know well that the reason he revealed himself
was to take away sins;
in him there is nothing sinful.
The man who remains in him does not sin.

The man who sins has not seen him
or known him.
Little ones,
let no one deceive you;
the man who acts in holiness is holy indeed,
even as the Son is holy.
The man who sins belongs to the devil,
because the devil is a sinner from the beginning.
It was to destroy the devil's works
that the Son of God revealed himself.

No one begotten of God acts sinfully
because he remains of God's stock;
he cannot sin
because he is begotten of God.
That is the way to see who are God's children,
and who are the devil's.
No one whose actions are unholy belongs to God,
nor anyone who fails to love his brother.
This, remember, is the message
you heard from the beginning:
we should love one another.
We should not follow the example of Cain
who belonged to the evil one
and killed his brother.
Why did he kill him?
Because his own deeds were wicked
while his brother's were just.
No need, then, brothers, to be surprised
if the world hates you.
That we have passed from death to life we know
because we love the brothers.
The man who does not love is among the living dead.
Anyone who hates his brother is a murderer,
and you know that eternal life
abides in no murderer's heart.
The way we came to understand love

was that he laid down his life for us;
we too must lay down our lives for our brothers.
I ask you, how can God's love survive in a man
who has enough of this world's goods
yet closes his heart to his brother
when he sees him in need?
Little children,
let us love in deed and in truth
and not merely talk about it.
This is our way of knowing we are committed to the
    truth
and are at peace before him
no matter what our consciences may charge us with;
for God is greater than our hearts
and all is known to him.
Beloved,
if our consciences have nothing to charge us with,
we can be sure that God is with us
and that we will receive at his hands
whatever we ask.
Why? Because we are keeping his commandments
and doing what is pleasing in his sight.
His commandment is this:
we are to believe in the name of his Son, Jesus Christ,
and are to love one another as he commanded us.
Those who keep his commandments remain in him
and he in them.
And this is how we know that he remains in us:
from the Spirit that he gave us.—1 John 3:1-24

26. Love of God Through Love of Neighbor

Beloved,
let us love one another
because love is of God;
everyone who loves is begotten of God
and has knowledge of God.

The man without love has known nothing of God,
for God is love.
God's love was revealed in our midst in this way:
he sent his only Son to the world
that we might have life through him.
Love, then, consists in this:
not that we have loved God,
but that he has loved us
and has sent his Son as an offering for our sins.
Beloved,
if God has loved us so,
we must have the same love for one another.
No one has ever seen God.
Yet if we love one another
God dwells in us,
and his love is brought to perfection in us.
The way we know we remain in him
and he in us
is that he has given us of his Spirit.
We have seen for ourselves, and can testify,
that the Father has sent the Son as savior of the world.
When anyone acknowledges that Jesus is the Son of
        God,
God dwells in him
and he in God.
We have come to know and to believe
    in the love God has for us.
God is love,
and he who abides in love
abides in God,
and God in him.
Our love is brought to perfection in this,
that we should have confidence on the day of
        judgment;
for our relation to this world is just like his.
Love has no room for fear;
rather, perfect love casts out all fear.

And since fear has to do with punishment,
love is not yet perfect in one who is afraid.
We, for our part, love
because he first loved us.
If anyone says, "My love is fixed on God,"
yet hates his brother,
he is a liar.
One who has no love for the brother he has seen
cannot love the God he has not seen.
The commandment we have from him is this:
Whoever loves God must also love his brother.
—1 John 4:7-21

27. The Greatest of These Is Love

Now I will show you the way which surpasses all the
others. If I speak with human tongues and angelic
as well, but do not have love, I am a noisy gong, a
clanging cymbal. If I have the gift of prophecy and,
with full knowledge, comprehend all mysteries, if I
have faith great enough to move mountains, but have
not love, I am nothing. If I give everything I have to
feed the poor and hand over my body to be burned,
but have not love, I gain nothing.

Love is patient; love is kind. Love is not jealous,
it does not put on airs, it is not snobbish. Love is never
rude, it is not self-seeking, it is not prone to anger;
neither does it brood over injuries. Love does not
rejoice in what is wrong but rejoices with the truth.
There is no limit to love's forbearance, to its trust, its
hope, its power to endure.

Love never fails. Prophecies will cease, tongues
will be silent, knowledge will pass away. Our knowledge is imperfect and our prophesying is imperfect.
When the perfect comes, the imperfect will pass away.
When I was a child I used to talk like a child, think
like a child, reason like a child. When I became a man

I put childish ways aside. Now we see indistinctly, as in a mirror; then we shall see face to face. My knowledge is imperfect now; then I shall know even as I am known. There are in the end three things that last: faith, hope, and love, and the greatest of these is love.—1 Corinthians 13:1-13

28. The Need and Reward of Repentance

Cry out full-throated and unsparingly,
    lift up your voice like a trumpet blast;
Tell my people their wickedness,
    and the house of Jacob their sins.
They seek me day after day,
    and desire to know my ways,
Like a nation that has done what is just
    and not abandoned the law of their God;
They ask me to declare what is due them,
    pleased to gain access to God.
"Why do we fast, and you do not see it?
    afflict ourselves, and you take no note of it?"
Lo, on your fast day you carry out your own pursuits,
    and drive all your laborers.
Yes, your fast ends in quarreling and fighting,
    striking with wicked claw.
Would that today you might fast
    so as to make your voice heard on high!
Is this the manner of fasting I wish,
    of keeping a day of penance:
That a man bow his head like a reed,
    and lie in sackcloth and ashes?
Do you call this a fast,
    a day acceptable to the LORD?
This, rather, is the fasting that I wish:
    releasing those bound unjustly,
    untying the thongs of the yoke;
Setting free the oppressed,

breaking every yoke;
Sharing your bread with the hungry,
   sheltering the oppressed and the homeless;
Clothing the naked when you see them,
   and not turning your back on your own.
Then your light shall break forth like the dawn,
   and your wound shall quickly be healed;
Your vindication shall go before you,
   and the glory of the LORD shall be your rear guard.
Then you shall call, and the LORD will answer,
   you shall cry for help, and he will say: Here I am!
If you remove from your midst oppression,
   false accusation and malicious speech;
If you bestow your bread on the hungry
   and satisfy the afflicted;
Then light shall rise for you in the darkness,
   and the gloom shall become for you like midday;
Then the LORD will guide you always
   and give you plenty even on the parched land.
He will renew your strength,
   and you shall be like a watered garden,
   like a spring whose water never fails.—Isaiah 58:1-11

29. Some Common Catholic Prayers

THE APOSTLES' CREED

I believe in God, the Father almighty,
  creator of heaven and earth.

I believe in Jesus Christ, his only Son, Our Lord.
  He was conceived by the power of the Holy Spirit
    and born of the Virgin Mary.
  He suffered under Pontius Pilate,
    was crucified, died, and was buried.
He descended to the dead.
On the third day he rose again.
  He ascended into heaven,
    and is seated at the right hand of the Father.
  He will come again to judge the living and the dead.

I believe in the Holy Spirit,
  the holy catholic Church,
  the communion of saints,
  the forgiveness of sins,
  the resurrection of the body,
  and the life everlasting.

THE OUR FATHER

Our Father, who art in heaven,
hallowed be thy name:
thy kingdom come;
thy will be done on earth as it is in heaven.
Give us this day our daily bread;
and forgive us our trespasses
as we forgive those who trespass against us;
and lead us not into temptation,

but deliver us from evil.

For the kingdom, the power, and the glory are yours
   now and for ever.

GLORY TO THE FATHER

Glory to the Father, and to the Son, and
      to the Holy Spirit:
   as it was in the beginning, is now, and will be for
      ever. Amen.

THE HAIL MARY

Hail, Mary, full of grace, the Lord is with you.
Blessed are you among women,
And blessed is the fruit of your womb, Jesus.
Holy Mary, Mother of God, pray for us sinners,
      now and at the hour of our death. Amen.

PART II

Guidelines for the Confessor

How to Use This Book

Together in Peace has been designed for practical use by confessor and penitent in the sacrament of Penance and for resource use by those who plan common penitential services either with or without sacramental absolution.

This confessor's edition includes:

Part I: The penitent's section exactly as it appears in a separate volume.

Part II: Advice for the priest on how to use this book, to construct an area of reconciliation or confessional room, to develop creative, personal penances and, finally, to cultivate the qualities of a good confessor.

Part III: The revised Rite of Penance.

Reconciling Individual Penitents

The penitent's portion of this text can be employed by the penitent alone or in conjunction with a willing confessor.

A. *The Penitent Alone*
In the first case, the penitent would simply follow the five-step process on his or her own. This would mean privately selecting the desired prayer (Step 1), scriptural reading(s) (Step 2), conscience point(s) (Step 3), then making the confession (Step 4), and last, executing the prescribed penance (Step 5). A confessor, however, aware the penitent has this book or making it easily available, could assign one of the scriptural passages located under Step 5 (pp. 73-100) and/or a creative, personal penance described in Chapter 2, pp. 124-130.

B. *The Penitent and Confessor Together*

In the second possibility, requiring a more lighted, open area like the room of reconciliation, the confessor would follow this procedure:

1. After the initial warm, human greeting, the penitent (and confessor) make a sign of the cross.

2. The confessor next prays with and for the penitent in his own words or employing one of the formulas below:

May God, who has enlightened every heart,   [42]
help you to know your sins
and trust in his mercy.

   The penitent answers:

Amen.

Or:

The Lord does not wish the sinner to die   [67]
but to turn back to him and live.
Come before him with trust in his mercy.
                        (Ezechiel 33:11)

Or:

May the Lord Jesus welcome you.   [68]
He came to call sinners, not the just.
Have confidence in him.   *(Luke 5:32)*

Or:

May the grace of the Holy Spirit   [69]
fill your heart with light,
that you may confess your sins with loving trust
and come to know that God is merciful.

Or:

May the Lord be in your heart [70]
and help you to confess your sins with true sorrow.

Or:

If you have sinned, do not lose heart. [71]
We have Jesus Christ to plead for us with the Father:
he is the holy One,
the atonement for our sins
and for the sins of the whole world. *(1 John 2:1-2)*

3. The priest then either by himself or with the penitent reads a scriptural passage found under Step 2, pp. 15-30. A list of brief biblical excerpts for this purpose or for memorization by the confessor can also be found on pp. 62-67, as part of the rite for individual penitents.

4. The penitent confesses his or her sins; the confessor offers the necessary counsel and proposes an appropriate satisfaction for the sins confessed. This penance, again, could be traditional prayers (found in Step 5) and/or a reading(s) located there and/or a creative, personal-type activity according to the principles and examples outlined in the section which follows.

If time and circumstances suggest this would be pastorally useful, the confessor could perform part of the penance, particularly the scriptural reading, with the penitent prior to absolution.

5. The penitent in his own words or according to one of the formulas given in Step 4 and aided by the confessor manifests his contrition.

6. The confessor, with his hands extended over the head of the penitent or at least with his right hand extended, proclaims the words of absolution:

God, the Father of mercies,   [46]
through the death and resurrection of his Son
has reconciled the world to himself
and sent the Holy Spirit among us
for the forgiveness of sins;
through the ministry of the Church
may God give you pardon and peace,
and I absolve you from your sins
in the name of the Father, and of the Son,+
and of the Holy Spirit.

The penitent answers:

Amen.

7. The confessor, finally alone or with the penitent, gives praise to the Lord for his mercy and dismisses the penitent in peace according to one of the formulas below which are also printed in Step 4 of the penitent's book.

Give thanks to the Lord, for he is good.   [47]

The penitent concludes:

His mercy endures for ever.

Then the priest dismisses the penitent who has been reconciled, saying:

The Lord has freed you from your sins. Go in peace.

Or:

May the Passion of our Lord Jesus Christ,   [93]
the intercession of the Blessed Virgin Mary
    and all the saints,
whatever good you do and suffering you endure,

110

heal your sins,
help you to grow in holiness,
and reward you with eternal life.
Go in peace.

Or:

The Lord has freed you from sin.
May he bring you safely to his kingdom in heaven.
Glory to him for ever.

Amen.

Or:

Blessed are those
whose sins have been forgiven,
whose evil deeds have been forgotten.
Rejoice in the Lord,
and go in peace.

Or:

Go in peace,
and proclaim to the world
the wonderful works of God,
who has brought you salvation.

Note: The priest by relying on his memory or spontaneous creativity could, of course, use many of these above steps even when the penitent confesses anonymously or in a darkened area where employment of this text, *Together in Peace,* is not feasible.

Reconciling Many Penitents With
Individual Confession and Absolution

This book may also serve as a resource text for those who plan the popular and desirable common or communal penance celebrations.

Chapter II in the new Rite of Penance (pp. 190-219 [#48-59]) contains the basic format and all alternative texts for reconciling many penitents with individual confession and absolution. Chapter IV supplies the complete list (#101-201) of biblical readings suggested for use in a group penance service and indicates where these texts can be found in this book.

Notice that the revised ritual (#55), following an earlier Vatican decree, directs the priest to absolve individually each penitent as he or she comes before him with his or her confession of sins.

The prayers, scriptural texts and examination of conscience points found in the penitent's part of *Together in Peace* could also, obviously, be incorporated into a communal penance service.

The Rest of This Book

The development of reconciliation rooms, creative, personal penances and, above all, good confessors are important, essential steps in the renewal of the sacrament of Penance. For that reason, we have included lengthy treatments of each topic in the pages which follow. Confessors would profit, also, by a reading of the ritual document's Introduction (pp. 165-189 [#1-40]).

Finally, for convenience's sake, we have reprinted the revised rite's Chapter III covering general absolution without individual confession (pp. 220-223 [#60-66]) and Appendix I of the rite which covers censures and irregularities (pp. 232-233).

Chapter 1
The Reconciliation Room

The environment which surrounds a liturgical celebration greatly influences its spiritual effectiveness.

In a negative way, for example, if participants are too hot or too cold, can't see the celebrant or hear the lector, they share less in the service and may even suffer a frustrating pain because of those obstacles.

More positively, the right use of color, light, seating arrangement and artistic decoration helps create a climate in which members of the community can pray much better.

A small weekday chapel, to illustrate, necessarily brings the few worshipers closer together. These persons then consciously or unconsciously sense in that situation that they form a Christian family and are praying, not as isolated individuals, but as a unit. Those same people in the larger, main church will tend to sit scattered around the nave and lose both the physical and spiritual togetherness experienced in the more compact chapel.

In similar fashion, the kind of place normally employed for Penance or Reconciliation can be a definite factor in determining how well or poorly penitents find Christ through this sacrament.

The revised ritual does not specify the type of area required or ideal for confession. Instead the Vatican decree leaves this to the judgment of bishops in each country. However, the rubric which directs a priest to hold his hands over the penitent's head (or at least his right hand) as he proclaims the words of absolution seems to allow an alternative for our customary confessional "boxes."

Several years ago at Holy Family Church in Fulton, New York, we prepared a room of reconciliation which would offer penitents a better atmosphere for the sacrament and an opportunity to confess easily in a variety of ways. This confessional room immediately bore great spiritual fruit and continues to justify the expense involved in its construction.[3]

One middle-aged man, sitting across the table from a priest in our new reconciliation room, made the following comment: "Father, it's harder to confess this way, but better." Like 75 per cent of the penitents who have used this area for the sacrament of Penance over the past few years, he opted for a face-to-face confession and found the experience a good one.

He was, however, under no pressure to confess in that way. Even entering and closing behind oneself the door of this recently completed room does not mean an irreversible decision to go face to face. Nor was the encouragement of such encounters the primary purpose in our mind when we began converting some spare office space off one church vestibule into a confessional room.

We were trying to create a more suitable environment for the sacrament of Penance. So often the traditional "boxes" are dark and cramped, making some feel closed in and others frightened. The box-type confessionals presume an unnatural whispering and normally preclude any visual contact between priest and penitent. Those who have trouble kneeling or wish to speak at length with the confessor must endure an awkward, uncomfortable, perhaps painful ordeal. Making confession a happy, peaceful meeting in faith with the merciful Jesus frequently becomes impossible simply because of the physical layout and atmosphere in which this dialogue takes place.

3. The following material is adapted from "A New Setting for Confession," by Joseph M. Champlin, "St. Anthony Messenger," November, 1972.

Environmentally, then, we wanted our room to express a simplicity of comfort, joy, quietness and dignity. But we also sought to provide three alternatives for persons seeking peace through penance: to confess anonymously, kneeling behind a grill; to confess behind this screen, but seated in a comfortable chair; to confess face to face in a conference area further into the room beyond the partition.

We contacted a liturgical artist, Mr. Robert Rambusch, to have some drawings prepared. Much of the work was done by volunteers from the parish. To break the windowless character of the space, two walls were painted in different, blending colors and the other two in off-white and matte. Wall-to-wall carpeting was laid to add warmth to the room.

Then a massive 5' x 7' wooden screen or grate, designed by Frederic Christian of the Rambusch firm, was constructed and bolted to the floor and one wall.

The screen serves a double function. First, it offers penitents the customary kneeling spot for confessions of that kind, yet with the advantage of actually seeing the priest through these inch-square apertures. In this arrangement a person no longer confesses to a blank wall or an opaque screen but to a confessor whose features are easily discernible. The penitent remains, however, unseen and is given further visual assurance of anonymity since the priest sits facing away from the grill.

Those unable to kneel with ease (e.g., pregnant women, persons advanced in age, individuals with lengthy confessions) may sit, still in the protected secrecy of that area, in a chair located next to the screen.

The screen also acts as a divider marking off two-thirds of the space as a conference section for face-to-face reconciliation. Upon entering the confessional room an individual feels an invitation to walk past the screen into this more brightly illumined, beautifully appointed portion.

The designers gave serious thought and great care to the question of lighting. The room used to be evenly lit by fluorescents, shadowless and uncomplimentary to the warmth of skin colors. Two incandescent floor lamps now provide a warm light there and simultaneously cast a subdued shadow over the screened confession area.

A rich 6' x 9' oriental rug in this section gives it a sense of unity and visually invites one into the space.

Mr. Christian suggested a handsome 3' x 3' table, imported from Switzerland, which gives the conference area a sense of place, a form to gather around. Two chairs and a small upright crucifix on the table complete the furnishings.

Those well versed in the art of counseling might object to the use of a table intervening between priest and penitent or question the straight, firm chairs and prefer soft, easy ones. To the contrary, our lengthy experience justifies the artist's recommendations.

Going to confession, even in face-to-face, conversational fashion, is not the same as seeking assistance from a guidance counselor or clinical psychologist. It's much easier to play games in the latter cases, although to do so would be an expensive and ultimately unproductive bit of recreation. Persons who seek the sacrament of penance do so presumably because they wish to reach God through his instrument, the priest. They know dishonesty with the confessor is tantamount to flaunting the Lord. In my 18 years as a priest I have witnessed few, perhaps no instances where a penitent seemed artificial or deceptive. People

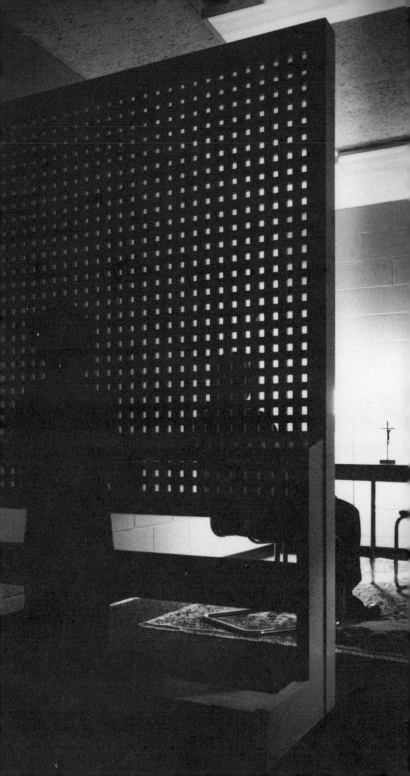

like that normally avoid the confessional experience.

My point here is this: a sinner searching for forgiveness and peace makes himself vulnerable, opens up, exposes a basically unpleasant part of himself. The person thinks: "I am not terribly happy with myself for doing this, thinking that, neglecting something else." Admitting fault and guilt to another human is hard enough, even brutal; to do so face to face requires added courage and means a further unveiling of the real me.

An encounter in the conference area of our confessional room must, consequently, create in some a sense of inner spiritual nakedness. The table eases that frightening feeling. It provides a place for the hands, something to hang on to, an object to hide behind.

The tiny table cross has become an unexpectedly potent part of the room. Our eyes speak volumes. The nervous penitent can't always look directly at the priest, especially in the early moments of a confession. So he glances here, there, everywhere: at the confessor, over his head, around the warm but plainly painted and decorated room; then, finally, the vision fixes on a body nailed to the cross. The crucifix says it all. "Father, forgive them . . . Greater love than this . . . I came to save sinners, not the just . . . Your sins are forgiven, go in peace. . . ."

Important to any architectural space, or room, is its entrance. We gave careful consideration to what symbol should be employed as an indication of the priest's presence. A thick (2½″) candle seemed best. It symbolizes Christ present in this sacrament of peace and recalls the paschal candle with its complex, multiple liturgical usage—for Holy Saturday and Eastertime, for baptisms and funerals, for death (to sin) and resurrection (to life).

Artist Paul Sisko produced the candleholder, an

angle of steel burned to a deep gunmetal color. Two pins on the bottom hold the nameplate of the priest hearing.

A crucial problem did arise soon after we began using the confessional room. The space, despite thick walls and a good-sized door, was not soundproof! Necessity spawns inventions and it proved creative here. I brought over my tape recorder and set it up in the vestibule, hoping through appropriate mood music (Mancini and Mozart) to neutralize voice sounds emanating from the room. It did that, but curious onlookers now wondered if we were taping confessions. This observation, once commonly held, certainly would frighten everyone away, so the next week I found the solution. An FM radio, placed in the vestibule, now plays uninterrupted and suitable music just loud enough to cover voices.

The presence of radio and table led us to another development. Why not keep pertinent literature in the vestibule waiting area? A few pamphlets and a paperback Bible could help people prepare. Several chairs would also make the sometimes lengthy wait less difficult.

Holy Family Church is four years old and done in modified contemporary style. Michael Ducar of the Rambusch Company designed some unique graphics for the door of our confessional room which correspond to the overall pattern of the building itself.

Several months before we finalized plans for the confessional room, some persons voiced a desire to memorialize former priests who had served in the parish. The message on this door fulfills that wish and also recalls verbally and visually the total dedication and faith present in the hearts of those who enter the room. It reads: "Dedicated to those of the parish whose ministry is to reconcile men to fellow man and man to God."

120

We continue to employ our confessional boxes on an alternate basis each Saturday. One priest hears in the room from 4 to 5 o'clock, the other in the box during that period. In the evening we reverse positions and on the next weekend similarly change the schedule. The previous Sunday parish bulletin carries details about who, when and where. A detachable sign, also made by our parishioner-artist, is placed before the box and points in the direction of the room indicating that, for example, "Father Tierney is hearing in the room off the northwest vestibule."

Two years ago a friendly reviewer of a book on the liturgy, *Christ Present and Yet to Come,* dismissed as "unreal" my concern about and recommendation of confessional rooms with a proper environment for the sacrament of Penance. Fortunately, our actual experience with this new space already has proved its merit. We have no statistics to substantiate an increase in the quantity of confessions, but my partner in the parish and I can definitely attest to an improvement in the quality of them. There is a greater openness, a concentration on the whole person and attitudes rather than upon specific acts and routine lists of repeated sins.

Moreover, in addition to the surprising number of people in every age bracket who choose to go face to face, there have been many positive testimonies from grateful penitents. I heard a teenage girl exclaim how open the room made her want to be; an individual in the later 40's remarked that he came because there was an opportunity to sit down and talk with the priest for confession; a grateful middle-aged woman admits that, if it were not for this room of reconciliation, she would never have summoned sufficient courage to make her peace with God after many years away from the sacrament of Penance.

Chapter 2

Creative and Personal Penances

The Council of Trent directed confessors to impose appropriate and healing penances ("satisfactiones") upon penitents according to the nature of the sins committed and the ability or disposition of the sinner. These, in the mind of those Church fathers, were to serve as reparation for past misdeeds, medicine for moral weakness and protection or assistance for a new life.

In customary Roman fashion, the reformed rite for this sacrament of Penance or reconciliation refers to that Tridentine document and builds on it. A section in its Introduction indicates the satisfaction required should fulfill those same basic purposes as sketched at Trent. However, there is within the current ritual more emphasis on the future and upon the conversion or renewal of the penitent.

The text cites St. Paul's example (Philippians 3:13): "Brothers, I do not think of myself as having reached the finish line. I give no thought to what lies behind but push on to what is ahead." The repentant sinner, consequently, should begin in a fresh way to live the mystery of Christ's salvation and move toward those things which are yet to come. Penances naturally ought to help in that task.

For various reasons confessors have, in the past years, for the most part tended to assign in confession only standard prayers as the satisfaction for one's sins. Priests today, on the other hand, more and more see the desirability of creative and personal penances in place of or as a complement to those traditional Our

Fathers and Hail Marys. They seek activities which bear a close link with the sins confessed and can thus serve as something of a carry-over into the days ahead.

I know from experience this is possible, but it demands patience, prudence and imagination:

Patience, because penitents, if asked, are normally slow or hesitant to suggest suitable penances on their own and frequently fail to grasp what the priest is attempting to accomplish.

Prudence, because confession for many or most continues to remain a somewhat awkward and nervous experience. Lengthy discussion about one's penance in the confessional or the assignment and acceptance of an unusual or complicated one can sometimes cause serious spiritual distress for the penitent.

Imagination, because the goal is to discover some task which in a very personal, yet clear and relatively simple way relates to the sin or sins confessed by that individual.

I requested some assistance in this area from three groups of public school children from our parish in my released time religious education classes (grades 7, 9, 12). They were asked to think for a 15-20 minute interval of some sins people commit and to suggest appropriate creative and personal penances for each. The results proved that certain persons, if given time and direction by a patient and prudent confessor, could even on their own recommend suitable satisfactions for misdeeds confessed.

A few samples of my pupils' imaginative efforts:

A seventh-grader recommended as a penance for missing Mass: go to Mass once during the week.

A ninth-grade student urged as satisfaction for speaking unkindly about someone: say some nice things about the person offended, both to that individual and to others.

A particularly keen and sensitive senior offered

this: "A father who finds it difficult to communicate with his children finally 'blew his top.' He was sorry for it, but could not tell them. A possible penance would be to sit down and tell his children, 'I love you.' That's all—just a simple and sincere 'I love you.' "

An optimistic junior high respondent thought that "keeping your room clean for a week or so" could be a fitting penance for the failure to obey one's parents.

The following table is not meant to revive the 7th-century Celtic tariff penances, but only to give confessors a few specific possibilities drawn from my own pastoral experiences and the creative efforts of those public school students.

It should be kept in mind that the best penance might be one suggested by the penitent himself or herself. Moreover, the task should be clear, not vague, concrete, not abstract, immediate, not of long-term duration, personal, yet not self-revelatory, difficult, but not excessively burdensome.

As we mentioned earlier, these may complement or replace the more conventional prayers. In addition, priests should not overlook the extensive selection of scriptural passages arranged in this book. There are distinct advantages to the confessor performing the penance with the penitent before proclaiming God's forgiveness. This becomes a rather convenient procedure, if one of the biblical excerpts is designated as part of or the entire satisfaction.

SIN	PENANCE
1. Miss Sunday or Holyday Mass	1. Go to Mass once during the week or Write a prayer in one's own words and recite it every day for a week, thus personally expressing worship of the Lord
2. Unkind and uncharitable words about another	2. Speak positively to that person or Be particularly friendly or considerate to the individual or Mention good points about him or her to others or Pray for the man or woman offended
3. Intemperance	3. Perform an act of self-denial or self-discipline
4. Infidelity	4. Do something to make up for that lack of loyalty—a gift for no special reason, dinner and an evening out, healing, complimentary words, say "I'm sorry" about another matter, respond warmly, offer to help around the house, show concern and interest in a facet of your partner's life, take the initiative in lovemaking
5. Swearing or irreverent use of God's name	5. Say "Jesus, Mary, Joseph" nine times or Prayerfully reflect on the gift of speech

SIN	PENANCE
6. Neglect of prayer	6. Spend a few quiet moments in church speaking to God in a personal way about this problem
7. Improper and selfish sex before marriage	7. Take a moment to consider the other individual as a person who should not be used for one's own pleasure or If serious about each other, on one occasion show your love in a different, less genital way—tell her she looks nice, do something he appreciates, give up what you would like to do for what your partner enjoys doing
8. Reading wasteful or harmful material	8. Read a chapter from the gospels or An article from a religious periodical
9. Sins of very young children	9. Kneel in church afterwards and in your own words thank God for forgiving you and ask him to help you be better
10. Past or present neglect of aging persons	10. Bake something or buy a few flowers, then visit a nursing home or hospital or house of an elderly individual
11. Talking back to your mother after she has had a rough day	11. Fix dinner for her or help with some of the housework

SIN	PENANCE
12. Talking back to your father after he has had a hard day	12. Wash the car for him or, in the winter, shovel the driveway and a path to the house
13. Fighting with your sister	13. If she is the same size, let her borrow a few of your clothes for a day or so; if not, let her borrow something else she would like to use
14. Fighting with your brother	14. Show an interest in his hobbies and offer to help him. If he plays football, throw a few with him
15. Envious of others	15. Visit a nursing home or someone who is in an unfortunate condition and count your own blessings
16. Lying	16. Admit your lie to the person deceived
17. Deceiving parents concerning one's whereabouts	17. The next time your friends are going someplace you know your parents wouldn't want you to go, stay home, then think about why you want to go there and why your parents don't want you to
18. Hurting others or fighting with them	18. Plan a party and invite them or Apologize and make up

19. Feeling sorry for yourself because of burdens or crosses	19. Study a crucifix for several minutes
	    or
	Make the stations of the cross
	    or
	Think about someone who has heavier burdens than you do

SIN	PENANCE
20. Greed or Selfishness	20. Drop something in the poor box
	or
	Send an offering to the missions
	or
	Give up a drink, a snack or a few cigarettes and use the money for a good cause
	or
	Listen patiently for a few extra minutes to someone you consider a bore, a pest or a waste of time

Chapter 3
The Role and Qualities of a Good Confessor

During a workshop at the 1974 Mile-Hi Religious Education Congress in Denver, I described our room of reconciliation at Holy Family and some of the experiences we have had with it.

A participant asked if this development in the sacrament of Penance did not imply confessors of the future would or should receive specialized training to prepare for their new role. My inquirer meant the equivalent of a master's degree in counseling or several advanced courses in psychology.

I replied that while such a formation might well prove helpful, the greatest need, in my opinion, was, is and will be priest-confessors who are prayerful, emotionally mature, loving, faith-filled, wise and understanding.

Upon hearing these comments, the audience broke into enthusiastic and sustained applause. The style and content of my lectures do not normally evoke such an outburst. I take that unusual reaction, then, as indicative of what penitents really look for in the priests who hear their confessions.

We have learned in the few years since introduction and implementation of the revised, flexible rites for Mass, Baptism, weddings, funerals and the like just how important is the celebrant's role.

131

The Bishops' Committee on the Liturgy, for example, in its statement on *Music in Catholic Worship*,[1] declares:

> Faith grows when it is well expressed in celebration. Good celebrations foster and nourish faith. Poor celebrations weaken and destroy faith.

We could simply extend this point and maintain: Good celebrants foster and nourish faith; poor celebrants weaken and destroy faith.

That document on music endorses such a conclusion and explicitly acknowledges the celebrant's critical importance in determining the spiritual effectiveness of a particular celebration. The words which follow pertain immediately to the Eucharist, but they apply with equal force to other liturgies, including the rite of Reconciliation:

> No other single factor affects the liturgy as much as the attitude, style, and bearing of the celebrant: his sincere faith and warmth as he welcomes the worshipping community: his human naturalness combined with dignity and sacredness as he breaks the Bread of Word and Eucharist.

The priest, therefore, can help penitents find Christ in this sacrament of peace or hinder them on their path to Jesus. His inner qualities and outer approach will, for better or for worse, greatly affect the kind of experience nervous, remorseful sinners have when they confess their failings.

I remember well trying to heal the wounds and rebuild the faith of a person who years earlier had stalked out of a confessional and muttered: "Never

---

1. USCC Publications, Washington, D. C., 1972.

again. I don't have to confess to a drunken priest."
After the dreadful encounter he, in fact, not only gave
up this sacrament, but stopped Sunday Mass attend-
ance as well.

Persons with strong faith can overlook serious
faults like that in celebrants and still find the Lord;
those with weaker faith cannot. The latter, deeply
hurt or angered or disillusioned, fall away for a few
months, a few years and sometimes, unfortunately, for
a lifetime.

Poor celebrants in these situations may destroy
people's faith. In other cases, they weaken it, a bad
enough effect even though the pain is not as deep
and the harm more easily repaired.

An elderly Ohio woman wrote these lines to me
after such a debilitating experience with one confessor
whose insensitivity and harshness crushed the troubled
lady.

> Father, you have no idea how rude and de-
> structive some priests are in the confessional.
>
> I am 68 years old and have a very confused
> mind from a fall over two years ago.
>
> I do not go to church when the weather is
> bad, but know if I called someone to take me, I
> could go even though I'm better off home.
>
> I've never missed Mass until I had my accident,
> so naturally I feel like confessing I missed Mass
> to have a clear conscience.
>
> The priest told me "I was wasting his time"
> by my confession about missing Mass and that I
> was lying. He told me I was a liar to confess I
> missed Mass because of the weather.
>
> I asked him not to confuse me, but he said
> I was already confused.
>
> When he kept insisting I was a liar and asked
> if I understood that, I told him I would accept it,

but didn't understand it.

I was given no penance and am not sure about absolution. I was so upset.

I prayed to God if I should go to Communion and finally did after a good act of contrition.

I have been told before I was wasting the priest's time, but to be called a liar, never.

Poor confessors can thus either destroy or weaken the faith of penitents. But, good confessors, on the other hand, can more positively, deeply nourish and strengthen it.

What follows is a list and description of qualities which should be present in the model confessor. Like the ideals of Jesus, these characteristics are, in effect, goals a priest strives for in his ministry more than results he regularly achieves in his efforts as a confessor.

A good confessor should be:

1. *Aware of his personal importance*

Father Gerald Broccolo, a young theologian from Mundelein Seminary in Chicago, has spoken frequently about how the celebrant's inner qualities are transparent and translucent. Those he leads in worship around the altar or who come to him for reconciliation sense instinctively and immediately he is or is not a man of prayer, faith, love and understanding.

Such qualities are communicated automatically and without effort on our part. The penitent can tell if we are content merely to perform a duty or are anxious to help a person. It makes a difference, as we have seen above.

The priest who grasps this and, further, who recognizes a responsibility to reveal God the Father's forgiving heart and to make present Jesus the Good

Shepherd will necessarily sense the importance of his work.

It is our Lord who saves, Christ who forgives, as we will note in a moment, but God does so through human instruments. Each priest conveys the loving mercy of Jesus in a unique way and no two of us are exactly alike. Every confessor not only exercises a divine function; he also does so in a humanly individualized manner.

The priest, conscious of both dimensions, cannot but take his task seriously.

2. A celebrator of Christ's forgiveness

We speak normally today about celebrating the Eucharist, the sacraments, the liturgy.

If we turn to natural celebrations like a wedding anniversary, a New Year's Eve dance or a birthday party for an understanding of the term, certain common elements come to mind: music, guests, preparation, host or hostess, food and drink, spontaneity, a definite ritual, remembrance of the past, joy, sorrow, love, community, speeches, a place, thoughts about the future.

Furthermore, celebrations presuppose a stepping aside from daily routines, an interrupting of our normal lives for a moment to place everything in perspective, to gain a long-range view.

With reservations and exceptions these characteristics apply to worship celebrations. However, the liturgy is a singular kind of celebration, a believing experience, a meeting with Christ in faith. We celebrate in liturgical worship the Paschal mystery of Jesus' coming, dying, rising, coming again.

Viewed in that fashion, we can speak about celebrating the sacrament. There is no rejoicing here over our sins, just as there is none over death at a Christian funeral. Our joyful celebration instead centers on the

135

power of Christ who by his resurrection has conquered death and sin.

The celebrant, consequently, needs to create and communicate in his exchange with the penitent a spirit of joy, a welcome home atmosphere, a warm acceptance of the wandering son who has returned to the father's house.

Chastising the sinner surely does not fit into this picture. A gentle firmness designed to stir the apathetic who seems to take the sacrament for granted or to have grown comfortable with an evil habit sometimes may prove necessary. But a confessor ought to tread carefully, speak softly and move cautiously when he feels a duty to correct in that manner.

This is, above all, a celebration of God's mercy and forgiveness.

3. *A man of faith*

Article 7 in the Constitution on the Sacred Liturgy describes the many presences of Christ in worship. He is present in the World, at Mass, in the Blessed Sacrament, when two or three gather for prayer, in the sacraments.

When a priest hears confessions, Christ hears them; when the confessor speaks, Jesus speaks; when the Church's representative pronounces words of healing forgiveness, our Lord pronounces them.

If the priest believes these truths, if those concepts have sunk deeply into his being, they will influence his way of life and his style as a confessor.

First of all, faith in Christ's presence throughout the reconciliation experience should give him a serene, humble confidence.

We are weak flesh and blood creatures. On a Saturday night after dinner, at the end of those marathon three-hour Holy Saturday sessions, during a period of special fatigue or illness, when preoccupied with other matters, we may just not be able physically, mentally or emotionally to respond with the perfect word, advice or penance. Furthermore, in complex, delicate questions we also often wonder what to say or if we have given the proper counsel.

Belief that it is Jesus who saves and speaks does not remove the responsibility we bear to do our best. It should, however, eliminate discouragement over our inadequacies, supply us with self-confidence in difficult issues and dissipate fretful "postmortems."

Second, faith in Christ's presence through this reconciliation encounter should lead the priest himself to a frequent use of that sacrament. If he does not often admit his own sins before God in the presence of a brother confessor, how can he encourage penitents to do so.

Most of us need to examine our consciences in that regard because priests' confessions have also declined over the past decade.

The distinguished theologian, Karl Rahner, suggests that monthly reception of this sacrament could be a good norm or guideline for persons seriously concerned about following Christ. I wonder how many of my readers have observed his principle in practice.

Third, faith in Christ's presence ought to make a priest particularly alert to the needs of brothers in the ministry who may wish to confess. When I telephone with the message: "Are you going to be in for a few minutes?" don't ask questions. Simply say "Yes," then rearrange, if possible, your schedule. It may not be reconciliation with God and forgiveness of sins I seek, but the possibility is always present and the situation extremely sensitive and significant.

Fourth, faith in the Lord's forgiving presence should create within the priest a constant readiness to hear any person's confession whenever asked. In a typically balanced fashion, the reformed ritual mentions that a confessor should always hold himself prepared and willing whenever the faithful reasonably request his services.

4. *A preacher of repentance*

Our faith also extends to the presence of Christ through the inspired words of sacred scripture. It is that belief, among other reasons, which has prompted the Church in its renewal of all the liturgical books to provide a rich selection of biblical passages for the celebration of every sacrament. The Order of Penance is no exception.

The penitent's edition of "Together in Peace" offers confessor and sinner 70 appropriate scriptural excerpts which can be employed in preparation and as penances. Their mutual faith will influence how much and the way both persons use those texts.

God's message in the Bible is at once a challenge and a comfort. We like to dwell on the sections which speak of our Lord's mercy and forgiveness, his promise of freedom and peace. But those passages are equally vital which call for repentance, a change of heart and the reform of one's life.

A priest as preacher must proclaim both messages. The introductory guidelines for this ritual expressly note that priests and bishops should summon through preaching God's word the faithful to a conversion or renewal of heart.

During my nearly two decades in the priesthood, I have preached several times every year, what I term my "Mary Magdalene sermon," especially prior to Christmas and Easter. The thrust is always a stress on Jesus' love for sinners and an encouragement to make that overdue confession, only the stories and illustrations vary.

Without fail those words from the pulpit will, in a week or a month, bring to me or to another priest someone who has long postponed the step, but finally gained courage through that homily.

A proclamation of this type, in addition to recounting one of the familiar "mercy" stories from scripture, should touch on certain ancient, but still real concerns of hesitant sinners: Can I be forgiven? Will the priest scold me? What do I say after so many years? Will the confessor reveal my sins to another or think less of me? How do I confess since I have forgotten the formula or do not have words to describe my sin? Is there hope for me even though my last was a bad confession? What if I continue to sin and fall back into my evil ways?

5. *Prayerful*

The ritual's preliminary principles direct a priest to acquire the knowledge and prudence necessary for a good confession, especially through prayer. Discernment of spirits, is, in the words of the Roman document, at once a gift of the Holy Spirit, the fruit of charity and an intimate understanding of God's word in the hearts of men.

The priest, then, who is serious about his reconciliation ministry must be a prayerful man both because penitents can sense the presence or absence of that essential characteristic within him and because he needs the Lord's help in executing his duties.

I offer at this point a few practical suggestions.

*Pray beforehand: At Mass on the day of confessions and before the tabernacle just prior to the task. One saint's words have been a favorite for me. "Lord, give me souls. Take away the other things."

*Pray with the penitent: The renewed format encourages personal prayer at the beginning of a confession, some response from the penitent and recommends, where feasible, a reading of God's word. There are six invitational texts published in the ritual, but it opens the possibility for confessors to speak in a personal, spontaneous and informal manner.

A prayer of that type might go something like this:

God our Father, send your Spirit upon this man; help him to see his sins; give him the courage to confess them and the faith to believe in Christ, your Son; let him experience your peace and freedom. We ask for these things in the name of Jesus, your Son and our brother. Amen.

If a confessor does not feel comfortable with something free or spontaneous, he can be equally effective by reading with a prayerful spirit one of the official greetings.

*Personalize the absolution: Prior to proclamation of the absolution formula, the priest might verbalize a prayer for the penitent which takes into consideration some of the sins confessed and leads into the Church's words of forgiveness.

For example, the confessor might pray along these lines on behalf of a married woman who is struggling with her relationship to an elderly mother-in-law:

Lord, pour your healing grace into this woman's heart. Give her patience to endure things beyond her control and the ability to accept people as they are, not as she wishes them to be. Now, through the words of your Church, forgive her. . . .

God, the Father of mercies, by the death and resurrection of his Son has reconciled the world to himself, and sent the Holy Spirit among us for the forgiveness of sins. Through the ministry of the Church may he give you pardon and peace. I absolve you. . . .

*Pray or read the penance with the penitent: When circumstances dictate (e.g., in a confessional room, at the rectory, on hospital calls), the priest could with the penitent pray one of the psalms or prayers given in the penitent's section of this book or read a scriptural passage printed in that portion of the booklet.

*Pray consciously, silently for a specific individual: In particularly difficult cases, the priest might pause a moment or two prior to speaking and ask the Lord in his heart for some guidance with the person before him.

*Ask penitents and parishioners to pray for you as a confessor: This may sound terribly pious, but prayers we do need and the request, sincerely made, conveys to others our humble, prayerful approach to this sacrament.

6. *A willing listener*

In today's depersonalized, committee-conscious, group-oriented, computerized society, the individual often is forgotten or loses a sense of identity. The sacrament of Penance, while designed to reconcile sinners with God, neighbor, one's own self and the world around, remains still an extremely intimate and personal experience. The confessor should recognize this and understand it may be one of the few occasions a penitent in our society has to talk at length about himself or herself.

As a standard procedure I have, from earliest days in the confessional, always offered a sinner an easy opportunity for this after the relation of sins. "Is there anything in your mind you would like to talk about?" That invitation, extended after their confession of faults and before any counseling remarks, has not always, nor even in the majority of occasions, been accepted. However, it lets penitents know you are disposed toward this; they may recall the offer and take advantage of it later in their lives when they do have a matter of importance and concern to discuss.

Contemporary counseling techniques stress the curative powers of effective listening. As authority persons accustomed to communicating grace and preaching doctrine, confessors need to be careful here. We must constantly evaluate our performance in the sacrament on the basis of updated theology and of truths uncovered by modern psychological science.

Did I too swiftly suggest a pat and ready-made solution? Talk too much? Did I listen? Fail to hear what the penitent really said? Did I forget that a few wise words will be heeded and remembered longer than many superficial ones?

Penitents generally do not seek specific resolutions of problems or answers to questions. Instead, they look for reassurance, confirmation that they made the correct decisions or are moving in the proper direction. After all, they have lived with the situation for some time and probably pondered the issue from every angle. Why should they expect us to grasp the total picture in a few seconds and instantly resolve the complex puzzle? Moreover, how can we presume that the power to proclaim God's forgiveness likewise enables us to dispense infallible guidance in every matter.

My first pastor, the late and venerable rector of the Syracuse Cathedral, Monsignor James P. McPeak, had frequent recourse to and made famous this turn-around question: "What do *you* think *you* ought to do about it?" A confessor could do worse than to use often that inquiry with his penitents.

7. *A holy person*

Just as the drunken priest and the insensitive confessor destroyed and weakened two penitents' faith, so a holy priest, like the faith-filled and prayerful one, can build up and deepen the sinner's inner life.

An elderly priest I know has, for many years, been the area's most popular confessor. The lines of penitents waiting for a few moments with him frequently stretch from altar rail to the church's entrance. Some in jest or cynicism credited his popularity to the fact that he supposedly couldn't hear, didn't understand or gave easy penances.

I always felt otherwise. For me the explanation rested in his unobtrusive, service-oriented personal holiness. People judged him a saint and, as in the life of the Savior he follows, power did and does go out from that saintly priest and heals all.

Holy priests are better confessors, true. But hearing confessions can also help priests become holier. The unsung and never to be revealed innocence and sanctity of so many lay persons or religious leaves us, at times, embarrassed that we have not tried harder or moved farther along the road to holiness.

8. Gentle and accepting

The biggest praise a penitent can offer the confessor is, in my view, the words: "You were very understanding." Not kind, which can be condescending, but understanding.

That encomium implies he accepted the sinner as a person. While of course not approving the sins confessed, neither did the priest reject this individual or somehow convey a belittling, scornful attitude toward him or her.

The tone of voice, facial expressions, questions asked and comments made all contribute here. We hope they convey Christ-like acceptance and badly needed gentleness.

A missionary told me early in my priesthood of his manner with penitents who either have been away from the sacrament for many years or obviously express great anxiety as they begin their confession. He would immediately interrupt them and say in a reassuring tone: "Now just relax, be at peace, take it easy, let me help you." I have followed his example and often will hear or note a perceptible sigh and release of tension.

Reflecting on our own failures and learning from confessional experiences can enable us to reflect the penitent's feelings back to him or to her. This is a particularly effective technique and makes the distressed individual sense we do understand the situation.

I always thought one of the Little Flower's unique gifts was her keen awareness of what sin is and does even though she had apparently never refused God anything from earliest years. Most of us, however, unfortunately acquire that sensitivity only through personal failures. In any event, phrases like "Do you feel so overwhelmed that you just don't think you can struggle any longer?" are potent words and with a little reassurance added on, become healing and helpful.

The priest who bellows, "You did what?" or becomes angry at a penitent's sins probably is manifesting some inner frustration of his own rather than saintly sorrow over wounds inflicted upon the Lord's Mystical Body.

Courageous penitents being subjected to a loud, harsh scolding might stop the confessor and say: "Father, I came here feeling like the woman caught in adultery and I thought you would be like Christ."

9. *Not afraid to bestow a healing touch*

The reformed rituals for several of our sacraments direct or suggest the celebrant or community physically touch a recipient.

For example: celebrant, parents and godparents sign the baby about to be baptized; the bishop imposes

144

hands upon candidates during ordination; a priest is to lay his hands upon the seriously ill prior to anointing; those who surround a dying Christian are encouraged to trace a cross on the forehead as a reminder of baptism and its promises.

So, too, in the revised Order of Penance a confessor should proclaim the Church's formula of absolution with both hands extended over the head of the penitent or at least with his right hand toward the person (No. 46). This is a visible, tangible sign of healing and reconciliation.

That gesture naturally is neither possible nor apparent to the penitent except in rooms of reconciliation described elsewhere in this booklet or in customary confessionals where the priest can be at least partially seen.

For those ordained ten or more years ago, this imposition of hands may seem strange and leave us somewhat uncomfortable. We were generally trained then to be physically aloof in our ministry and Jesus' command after the resurrection, "Noli me tangere," was cited by instructors when they urged caution, reserve and distance.

Implementation of the new directive requires warmth and common sense. I have not found it very feasible to impose hands upon the head of a penitent sitting across from me in the confessional room. On the other hand, it is rather natural (perhaps more contemporary) to clasp a person's hand or hands or arm during a prayer prior to absolution or immediately before he leaves the area.

Much depends on the particular penitent and the mood of the moment. For some, this physical gesture would be a wonderful sign of forgiveness, reconciliation and acceptance. For others, its newness could cause misunderstanding and create further tension in a sacramental situation already filled with anxiety.

The confessor, open to the Holy Spirit and sensitive to the disposition of his penitent, must judge each person separately and may make a few mistakes in the process.

We need to preach occasionally about this development, its purpose and historical basis. That will greatly alleviate the confessor's burden as penitents come gradually to understand and accept the rite.

However, even after the imposition of hands becomes standard procedure, it will remain an extremely personal gesture. Some priests will execute it easily and warmly; others will do so with difficulty and in a wooden way. Those confessors who feel they fit into the latter category should not despair. Their inner sincerity will come through despite the seeming awkwardness of the external action. And, lest we forget, it is Christ who forgives and acts through us.

While certain priests may need to push themselves into a more physical, touching manner of healing sinners, others may find they must restrain a natural effusiveness which can alienate.

Both types of confessors obviously should be on guard in those charged circumstances when a troubled penitent might misconstrue the imposition of hands. Lonely, injured spouses or sexually immature individuals could see this as a kind of an advance. While a sympathetic priest may feel compelled to comfort and console, he should be aware that his well-intentioned action may instead confuse and complicate.

Attractive, substantial stoles (not the traditional pocket variety) with appropriate designs can form a part of this modified imposition of hands. One of our sisters, confined in a hospital, knitted such a vestment for me. It bears the word, "Peace," on one arm, a Chi-Rho on the other.

10. *Careful to prepare mind and body*

Father Nicholas Weber, the Jesuit who travels with his circus throughout the United States and teaches liturgy on the West Coast, stresses the need for performers in liturgy to prepare properly for the celebration. This includes adequate physical rest.

Most of us have occasionally stayed up too long with the late show, then struggled wearily through Mass and teaching and appointments the next day. We were not operating at peak efficiency, knew it, regretted the imprudence and resolved to retire earlier. The good intentions are sometimes short-lived.

Hearing confessions requires greater concentration and thus freshness than perhaps any other sacramental ministry. It demands, therefore, we enter the box or room fairly rested and alert. Preconfessional-hour afternoon naps have become a regular part of my life, and I have no qualms about them. Better this than a painful, nodding, foggy session with penitents.

The increasing face-to-face possibilities with this sacrament make such preparation more imperative. In these encounters penitents can see you are tired and sluggish; in the other arrangement, they can only guess you are.

In addition to the proper anticipatory care of his body, the confessor will discharge his function more satisfactorily if he also prepares his mind for the task. With a few new ideas from the Bible, the day's liturgy or recent reading in his thoughts, he can offer some fresh encouragement and avoid slipping back into worn-out, trite and repetitive phrases.

11. *Eager to involve penitents, but not in a burdensome way*

Other sections of this book give practical suggestions for involvement of penitents in the confessional dialogue. They include scriptural readings, commonly recited or read penitential passages, and the development of imaginative, personal penances.

While such engagement is praiseworthy and often productive, we must be careful our efforts to involve do not create a burden for those not receptive to such ideas.

Spending long, painful moments in an attempt to agree on some innovative penance can prove counterproductive. The penitent may recall only the ordeal (remember they usually kneel; we sit), not the penance. Moreover, the resulting activity could be so complicated and elusive the poor person wonders what it was or when it could be performed.

Similarly, leading, searching interrogations easily communicate the impression of a meddlesome intruder rather than an interested friend.

Not every Catholic Christian wishes confession to be a face-to-face, lengthy, involved, highly personal experience. Some prefer a brief, in-and-out event stripped of accidentals and limited to the bare essentials. Confessors may wish to change their views and enrich these encounters. But if he alienates the penitents, his efforts will prove fruitless and they will, in the future, either avoid him or the sacrament itself.

"Quidquid recipitur, per modum recipientis recipitur." We can only be of service to others to the extent they wish us to help and are open to our suggestions.

12. *Conscientious*

One hears too frequently these days the anguished complaint of penitents who made a "devotional" confession and were cut down by the priest with the rebuke of "wasting my time."

Perhaps that trend explains the Holy See's admonition in its June 16, 1972, "Pastoral Norms Concerning the Administration of General Sacramental Absolution": "Priests should be careful not to discourage the faithful from frequent or devotional confession. On the contrary, let them draw attention to its fruitfulness for Christian living."

It refers then to this passage from the 1943 encyclical letter on the Mystical Body of Christ:

The same result would follow the opinions of those who assert that little importance should be given to the frequent confession of venial sins. Of far greater importance, they say, is that general confession which the spouse of Christ surrounded by her children in the Lord makes each day by the mouth of the priest as he approaches the altar. It is true indeed, venerable brothers, that venial sins may be expiated in many ways which are to be highly commended. But to hasten daily progress along the path of virtue we wish the pious practice of frequent confession to be earnestly advocated. Not without the inspiration of the Holy Spirit was this practice introduced into the Church. By it genuine self-knowledge is increased, Christian humility is developed, bad habits are corrected, spiritual neglect and tepidity are countered, the conscience is purified, the will is strengthened, salutary self-control is obtained, and an increase of grace is secured by the very fact that the sacrament is received. Let those, therefore, among the younger clergy who make light of or weaken esteem for frequent confession realize that what they are doing is foreign to the Spirit of Christ, and disastrous for the mystical body of our Savior.[2]

2. "Mystical Body of Christ," paragraph 86, National Catholic Conference News Service translation, appearing in "The New Liturgy," by R. Kevin Seasoltz, Herder and Herder, New York, 1966, p. 93.

Those legal and doctrinal principles, translated into pragmatic recommendations for priests, could read like this:

Be on time.

Stay in the confessional until the scheduled hours are completed.

Experiment to determine what are the most convenient confession hours for penitents.

Make yourself available for confessions during wakes on the night before a funeral.

Give parents of First Communicants easy accessibility to the sacrament.

Prepare parents and children well for First Confession.

Remember how effectively sickness and hospital beds convert sinners and lead them to repentance.

Publish in the Sunday bulletin your willingness to hear the confession of anyone at anytime in any place.

13. *Willing to give penitents the benefit of a doubt*

As celebrants we are, especially in these days, called upon to make some delicate decisions. Should we baptize the child of nonpracticing Catholic parents? What kind of a religious ceremony, if any, ought we to provide for an engaged couple who have not for several years participated in Sunday Mass and do not intend to change that pattern in the foreseeable future? Do we officiate at the wedding of a 17-year-old pregnant girl and her 18-year-old fiance?

Similar dilemmas face the confessor. A stern, strict approach may forever turn the weak person away from this sacrament. On the other hand, a soft, easy attitude might keep the penitent from coming to grips with the situation and making a vital effort to reform.

There is no question that firmness on the priest's part sometimes brings penitents to a new life. But that procedure involves great risks, constitutes a kind of spiritual brinkmanship, and should be employed only with extreme care and caution.

I think as a general rule the priest might, instead, seek to keep alive the barely flickering flame of faith and love in a sinner's heart by tender treatment rather than totally to snuff it out by a discouraging harshness.

Why does a penitent come to confession in the first place unless there exists in the heart a basic sorrow for sin and a desire to change? Should we not presume that a person, regardless of past failures and the current situation, hopes the sacrament of Penance will somehow help remove this sin's stranglehold on him or her? Can we not give each individual confessing the benefit of a doubt? In dubious circumstances, would it not be better to raise a few hard questions, proclaim the Lord's forgiveness and leave the uncertain case in a merciful God's hands?

Reasonably refusing absolution is, of course, within the confessor's competence. But it devastates the penitent and, in my judgment, rarely, if ever, should be done.

14. *Conscious he represents the Church*

Several years ago, at the height of the controversy over our Holy Father's encyclical "Humanae Vitae," a woman in deep distress over this aspect of her married life came to me for advice. She had sought help from a confessor in resolving the conflict between what her conscience seemed to urge and what she thought the papal document taught with regard to artificial contraception.

The priest lightly dismissed her anxiety and reportedly said there was no problem here since he disagreed with the pope on this matter. His answer just further confused the lady. She came hoping to find a way of remaining loyal to the Church while following the dictates of her conscience. The confessor's disloyal remark totally destroyed his credibility as far as she was concerned and failed to ease her burden.

The new ritual's introductory principles touch on this point. Article 9 mentions that priests, in exercising their task of reconciliation, do so in communion with the bishop and share both his power and responsibility as chief moderator of the penitential discipline.

That statement recalls the early Christian practice in which a bishop actually did reconcile sinners publicly and readmit them to the worshiping community.

The confessor, consequently, must act with an awareness he speaks for and in the name of the Church. His role transcends personal warmth and understanding even though those qualities are presumed for the task. We proclaim that God has and does forgive, is now forgiving. But we announce that mercy "per ministerium Ecclesiae" and absolve in the name of the Father, the Son, and the Holy Spirit (renewed form).

A priest, however, can teach faithfully what the Church believes without imputing sin to the penitent kneeling or sitting before him. It is one thing to state Catholic teaching, quite another to accuse the individual. Sin remains a personal conscience matter between God and the penitent. We can judge as priests only by surface actions or as confessors merely to the extent persons reveal their inner selves. Most of us need occasionally to remember our limitations in this regard.

Loyalty to the Church does not mean a slavish concern for disciplinary ecclesiastical laws. As in other liturgical celebrations, the confessor should blend a healthy regard for the rubrics with a commonsense application of them to the ever variable situations of real life. Dealing with reserved cases, hearing women's confessions in the rectory without a screen, insisting on integrity in awkward circumstances or with troubled penitents ought not to cause undue concern in the priest's mind.

Canon law has always been more flexible and down to earth than most American Catholics appreciate. In the majority of instances, a section of the Code covers in theory what the priest decides must be carried out in practice.

"Lex suprema est salus animarum," "Do the best you can," "Sacramenta sunt propter homines," and "Liturgy is for the people, not people for the liturgy" —four principles I enunciated in another book hold true when ministering the sacrament of Penance.

15. *Emotionally and spiritually mature in his approach*

An emotionally mature person knows how to control time, temper, eating, drinking, sexual drives. Moreover, that individual has self-confidence, is not insecure, can adapt to changing circumstances and adjust to various kinds of people. Such a grown-up person accepts criticism without becoming hostile or defensive and does not grow jealous of others in similar positions. People like this do not work out their own needs through the problems of others.

A spiritually mature person works from a pure heart, never manipulates people, is not on an ego trip and has the good of others in view.

Those descriptive characteristics applied to the confessor might result in these practical conclusions:

*Always have the confessor's name clearly displayed in the reconciliation area. Penitents possess the right to select or avoid specific priests.

153

*When several priests alternate periods in the confessional, the weekly bulletin should indicate, if possible, who is hearing where and when.

*A priest ought to foster within his penitents a sense of freedom, freedom to return to him if they wish or to seek another confessor at any time for whatever reason. Encouraging dependency is neither a Christian virtue nor helpful for personal growth.

*The confessor whose lines are short by comparison or who learns a favorite parishioner goes to another priest should fight the tendency to feel sad or envious. Why penitents choose one confessor over another or why a particular priest enjoys popularity is a great mystery known ultimately to the Lord alone.

Individuals do frequently transfer their feelings to other persons for various conscious and unconscious reasons. Priests, in virtue of their position, often are the targets for such transference, especially as they labor in the confessional. Recognition of this point should aid a confessor in understanding why certain penitents may come to him personally and others seek another.

A priest really should spend little or no time analyzing this phenomenon except for a swift review of his own performance in the confessional. Perhaps he has developed an approach that alienates penitents; it is more likely, however, that he will discover no explanation and would do well to forget about the matter.

Confessors with pure, generous, mature hearts simply go about the task aware that God works through a rich variety of numerous instruments. Each priest will touch certain individuals who can be reached by no other confessor. Some persons find this priest helpful for a time and then feel the need for a change. Christ seems to act in abundance through one confessor and in more limited fashion through another.

The Church, we know, has many members and each person contributes a share to the Body's well-being as the Spirit sees fit. As long as we pray, are available, and conscientiously care for the one person before us, our hearts should be at peace. We have done our part.

*Don't undermine another priest's confessional words or approach. When a penitent reports that "Father so and so said this" and the advice seemed improper or unwise, a mere "You probably misunderstood him" will usually take care of it. The confessor can then move on and rectify the situation without prejudice to the previous priest. After all, he is unable to defend himself.

16. *Careful about confidentiality*

The renewed ritual reminds priests that as God's ministers they learn the innermost secrets of a person's conscience and, consequently, are bound by their office to preserve with utmost concern the sacramental seal of confession.

Few confessors need a reminder about this. The history of confidentiality in the sacrament of Penance is a remarkably good one.

Recent court cases suggest we might in future years be put to the test in this area. That remains to be seen.

The increment in face-to-face encounters, however, does inject a new difficulty in observing the confessional seal. Penitents tend in that arrangement to bring up details connected with, but removed from the sins confessed. In addition, the priest often actually knows the person's identity.

This, therefore, requires a bit of extra caution. Information not under the seal, but learned within the confessional context and mentioned outside the sacrament might convey the impression confidentiality has been betrayed when in fact it has not.

17. *Wise and delicate with children*

The fewer words, greater meaning principle applies with special force to young preteen children in the sacrament of Penance.

A few phrases about God's love for them and his delight at their presence in the confessional will probably prove more beneficial than extremely specific advice about a fault or virtue.

Similarly, as we mentioned in another section, general penances for the very young ("spend a few minutes thanking God for being so good to you and asking him to help you be better") are normally preferable to precise prayers like the Our Father or Hail Mary.

Despite their few years, children in those early grades have minds of their own. For that reason adults, whether priests, teachers or parents, should give these youthful penitents freedom in the selection of confessors and in the manner of confessing.

Dad and mother certainly must offer the good example of frequent confessions and may find it occasionally necessary to remind their offspring of the sacrament, even to push them gently in that direction. However, the value of group pressure from clergy or teachers similar to that which used to be common in Catholic schools on the eve of First Fridays remains open for debate. Likewise, insistence by priests that every child must confess before First Communion runs contrary to the Vatican decree and invades the parents' rightful domain.

18. *Dignified in the use of the sacramental words and symbols*

These words and gestures have power in themselves, but they take on added meaning and exert greater impact when spoken or executed with care. Some recommendations about the new rite in this connection follow below:

*A reverent sign of the cross made with the penitent in the beginning and over the person during the absolution formula.

*Slow and sincere recitation of the introductory prayer.

*A stole of substance and beauty.

*Patient encouragement while the penitent recites a prayer of contrition.

*Strong, warm, healing imposition of hands where possible.

*Personalization of the forgiveness form when the penitent clearly and willingly identifies himself or herself in the course of the confession. "I absolve you, N, from your sins. . . ."

*Active verbal involvement of the penitent in the proclamation of praise and dismissal rite, if feasible.

19. *One who heals*

Penitents and priests involved with the charismatic renewal movement see in the sacrament of Penance a unique manifestation of the Holy Spirit's influence and believe God's power can marvelously heal, deliver and strengthen through this confessional experience.

Father Michael Scanlan, T.O.R., former seminary rector and now President of Steubenville (Ohio) College, has developed these ideas in a small, but very popular booklet entitled *The Power in Penance*.[3] I

3. Michael Scanlan, T.O.R., *The Power in Penance,* Ave Maria Press, Notre Dame, Indiana, 1972.

would recommend the volume to priests. Those immersed in charismatic activities probably already are familiar with the book, or at least its approach to confession; those not, should become aware of such a new and different dimension to the sacrament described in it.

The author wrote the text a few years prior to approval and publication of the revised ritual for this sacrament of reconciliation. However, the reformed format is so flexible that with a few minor adjustments the procedure he suggests could easily be worked into that authorized rite. Moreover, the penitent's material and confessor's guidelines contained within *Together in Peace* fit rather naturally into his recommended style.

In a word, what he proposed from experience and in a pioneering way does not conflict with either the revised Roman rite or this particular text. On the contrary, they complement one another. A few illustrations should make the point.

Father Scanlan describes a process he terms the identification and confirmation of difficulty. This seeks to determine, through faith, prayer and attentive listening to promptings of the Holy Spirit what is the "base or root of the sin," what is "causing you to sin and blocking your growth in union with God."

He suggests a penance which flows logically from the nature of the confession and mentions a gospel text on healing as appropriate.

The Franciscan writer stresses, also, the laying on of hands upon the head of the penitent when practical and cites instances in which priests have experienced a sense of power flowing through their hands on these occasions.

Finally, he outlines prayers of healing, deliverance and strengthening offered by the priest for the penitent following the absolution.

Priests who read through the five-step process in the penitent's section of *Together in Peace* and the principles in this section of the confessor's edition will recognize how Father Scanlan's proposals either already form part of the new rite or can be incorporated quite simply into it.

For an even more current work about the subject of healing from a charismatic viewpoint, readers might consult Father Francis MacNutt's latest volume, *Healing*.[4] He treats the matter at length and indicates how this development in the Church easily can be adapted into the revised ritual for Penance.

20. *Communicator of the Sacred*

Roman Catholic worship contains a heavy dose of sacred symbols—bread and wine, oil, water, imposition of hands. In fact, the liturgy is essentially symbolic, if we properly understand the term.

The God we adore stands above and beyond us even while close and present in our midst. Transcendent, wholly other, the one beyond are words or phrases we frequently employ to describe the Lord who said, "I AM."

In the liturgy, then, we attempt to communicate the fundamentally incommunicable. For human words cannot adequately describe nor our minds fully grasp the Almighty. Jesus, as *the* perfect sign or sacrament, makes the task easier, but there, too, we fail in totally comprehending the mystery of Christ who is Savior, Lord, God, man.

Symbols help. They lead us to the mystery, give us a glimpse or taste of it, while not allowing complete possession. Through sacred symbols (think of

---

4. Francis MacNutt, O.P., *Healing,* Ave Maria Press, Notre Dame, Indiana, 1974.

the Eucharist), we recall the past, experience God's presence, and look to the future.

The sacrament of Reconciliation or Penance works in similar fashion. Its holy signs (words and hands) remind us of God's loving mercy over centuries of salvation history, and make that forgiveness, healing and reconciliation present to us now, and pledge perfect wholeness at the second coming.

To paraphrase words from the ritual's Introduction: the celebrant, in pronouncing the words of absolution, indicates the sinner's reconciliation proceeds from God's mercy, is connected with Christ's Paschal mystery, results from the Holy Spirit's intervention and takes place through the ministry of the Church.

Sacred realities, these, to be communicated in a holy way by a sacred person, a set-aside, consecrated celebrant of God's peace-giving sacrament.

PART III
Rite of Penance

PART III: RITE OF PENANCE

SACRED CONGREGATION FOR DIVINE WORSHIP

Decree

Reconciliation between God and men was brought about by our Lord Jesus Christ in the mystery of his death and resurrection (see Romans 5:10). The Lord entrusted the ministry of reconciliation to the Church in the person of the apostles (see 2 Corinthians 5:18ff). The Church carries this ministry out by bringing the good news of salvation to men and by baptizing them in water and the Holy Spirit (see Matthew 28:19).

But because of human weakness, Christians "turn aside from [their] early love" (see Revelation 2:4) and even break off their friendship with God by sinning. The Lord, therefore, instituted a special sacrament of penance for the pardon of sins committed after baptism (see John 20:21-23), and the Church has faithfully celebrated it throughout the centuries—in varying ways, but retaining its essential elements.

The Second Vatican Council decreed that "the rite and formulas of penance are to be revised in such a way that they may more clearly express the nature and effects of this sacrament."[1] In view of this the Congregation for Divine Worship has carefully prepared a new *Rite of Penance* so that the celebration of the sacrament may be more fully understood by the faithful.

In this new rite, besides a *Rite for Reconciliation of Individual Penitents,* a *Rite for Reconciliation of Several Penitents* has been drawn up to emphasize the relation of the sacrament to the community. This rite places individual confession and absolution in the context of a celebration of the word of God. Furthermore, for special occasions a *Rite for Reconciliation of Several Penitents with General Confession and Absolution* has been composed in accordance with the Pastoral Norms on General Sacramental Absolution, issued by the Congregation for the Doctrine of the Faith on June 16, 1972.[2]

The Church is solicitous in calling the faithful to continual conversion and renewal. It desires that the baptized who have sinned should acknowledge their sins against God and their neighbor and have heartfelt repentance for them, and it tries to prepare them to celebrate the sacrament of penance. For this reason the Church urges the faithful to attend penitential celebrations from time to time. The Congregation has therefore made regulations for such celebrations and has proposed examples or specimens which episcopal conferences may adapt to the needs of their own regions.

Accordingly Pope Paul VI has by his authority approved the *Rite of Penance* prepared by the Congregation for Divine Worship and ordered it to be published. It is to replace the pertinent sections of the *Roman Ritual* now in use. The rite in its Latin original is to come into force as soon as it is published, but vernacular versions will be effective from the day determined by the episcopal conferences, after they have approved the translation and received confirmation from the Apostolic See.

Anything to the contrary notwithstanding.

From the office of the Congregation for Divine Worship, Dec. 2, 1973, the First Sunday of Advent.

> By special mandate of the Pope
> Jean Cardinal Villot
> Secretary of State
> +Annibale Bugnini
> Titular Archbishop of Diocletiana
> Secretary of the Congregation for Divine
>   Worship

1. Second Vatican Council, constitution *Sacrosanctum Concilium*, no. 72: *AAS* 56 (1964), p. 118.
2. See *AAS* 64 (1964), pp. 510-514.

RITE OF PENANCE

Introduction

I. THE MYSTERY OF RECONCILIATION IN THE HISTORY OF SALVATION

1. The Father has shown forth his mercy by reconciling the world to himself in Christ and by making peace for all things on earth and in heaven by the blood of Christ on the cross.[1] The Son of God made man lived among men in order to free them from the slavery of sin[2] and to call them out of darkness into his wonderful light.[3] He therefore began his work on earth by preaching repentance and saying: "Turn away from sin and believe the good news" (Mark 1:15).

This invitation to repentance, which had often been sounded by the prophets, prepared the hearts of men for the coming of the Kingdom of God through the voice of John the Baptist who came "preaching a baptism of repentance for the forgiveness of sins" (Mark 1:4).

Jesus, however, not only exhorted men to repentance so that they should abandon their sins and turn wholeheartedly to the Lord[4], but he also welcomed sinners and reconciled them with the Father.[5] Moreover, by healing the sick he signified his power to forgive sin.[6] Finally, he himself died for our sins and rose again for our justification.[7] Therefore, on the night he was betrayed and began his saving passion,[8] he instituted the sacrifice of the new covenant in his blood for the forgiveness of sins.[9] After his resurrection he sent the Holy Spirit upon the apostles, empowering them to forgive or retain sins[10] and sending them forth to all peoples to preach repentance and the forgiveness of sins in his name.[11]

The Lord said to Peter, "I will give you the keys of the kingdom of heaven, and whatever you bind on earth will be bound in heaven, and whatever you loose on earth will be loosed also in heaven" (Matthew 16:19). In obedience to this command, on the day of Pentecost Peter preached the forgiveness of sins by baptism: "Repent and let every one of you be baptized in the name of Jesus Christ for the forgiveness of your sins" (Acts 2:38).[12] Since then the Church has never failed to call men from sin to conversion and by the celebration of penance to show the victory of Christ over sin.

2. This victory is first brought to light in baptism where our fallen nature is crucified with Christ so that the body of sin may be destroyed and we may no longer be slaves to sin, but rise with Christ and live for God.[13] For this reason the Church proclaims its faith in "the one baptism for the forgiveness of sins."

In the sacrifice of the Mass the passion of Christ is made present; his body given for us and his blood shed for the forgiveness of sins are offered to God again by the Church for the salvation of the world. In the eucharist Christ is present and is offered as "the sacrifice which has made our peace"[14] with God and in order that "we may be brought together in unity"[15] by his Holy Spirit.

Furthermore our Savior Jesus Christ, when he gave to his apostles and their successors power to forgive sins, instituted in his Church the sacrament of penance. Thus the faithful who fall into sin after baptism may be reconciled with God and renewed in grace.[16] The Church "possesses both water and tears: the water of baptism, the tears of penance."[17]

II. THE RECONCILIATION OF PENITENTS
IN THE CHURCH'S LIFE

The Church Is Holy but Always in Need of Purification

3. Christ "loved the Church and gave himself up for her to make her holy" (Ephesians 5:25-26), and he united the Church to himself as his bride.[18] He filled her with his divine gifts,[19] because she is his body and fullness, and through her he spreads truth and grace to all.

The members of the Church, however, are exposed to temptation and unfortunately often fall into sin. As a result, "while Christ, 'holy, innocent, and unstained' (Hebrews 7:26) did not know sin (2 Corinthians 5:21) but came only to atone for the sins of the people (see Hebrews 2:17), the Church, which includes within itself sinners and is at the same time holy and always in need of purification, constantly pursues repentance and renewal."[20]

Penance in the Church's Life and Liturgy

4. The people of God accomplishes and perfects this continual repentance in many different ways. It shares in the sufferings of Christ[21] by enduring its own difficulties, carries out works of mercy and charity,[22] and adopts ever more fully the outlook of the Gospel message. Thus the people of God becomes in the world a sign of conversion to God. All this the Church expresses in its life and celebrates in the liturgy when the faithful confess that they are sinners and ask pardon of God and of their brothers and sisters. This happens in penitential services, in the proclamation of the word of God, in prayer, and in the penitential aspects of the eucharistic celebration.[23]

In the sacrament of penance, the faithful "obtain

from the mercy of God pardon for their sins against him; at the same time they are reconciled with the Church which they wounded by their sins and which works for their conversion by charity, example, and prayer."[24]

Reconciliation with God and with the Church

5.   Since every sin is an offense against God which disrupts our friendship with him, "the ultimate purpose of penance is that we should love God deeply and commit ourselves completely to him."[25] Therefore, the sinner who by the grace of a merciful God embraces the way of penance comes back to the Father who "first loved us" (1 John 4:19), to Christ who gave himself up for us,[26] and to the Holy Spirit who has been poured out on us abundantly.[27]

"By a hidden and loving mystery of God's design men are joined together in the bonds of supernatural solidarity, so much so that the sin of one harms the others just as the holiness of one benefits the others."[28] Penance always entails reconciliation with our brothers and sisters who are always harmed by our sins.

In fact, men frequently join together to commit injustice. It is thus only fitting that they should help each other in doing penance so that freed from sin by the grace of Christ they may work with all men of good will for justice and peace in the world.

The Sacrament of Penance and its Parts

6.   The follower of Christ who has sinned but who has been moved by the Holy Spirit to come to the sacrament of penance should above all be converted to God with his whole heart. This inner conversion of heart embraces sorrow for sin and the intent to lead a new

life. It is expressed through confession made to the Church, due satisfaction, and amendment of life. God grants pardon for sin through the Church, which works by the ministry of priests.[29]

a) Contrition

The most important act of the penitent is contrition, which is "heartfelt sorrow and aversion for the sin committed along with the intention of sinning no more."[30] "We can only approach the Kingdom of Christ by *metanoia*. This is a profound change of the whole person by which one begins to consider, judge, and arrange his life according to the holiness and love of God, made manifest in his Son in the last days and given to us in abundance" (see Hebrews 1:2; Colossians 1:19 and *passim*).[31] The genuineness of penance depends on this heartfelt contrition. For conversion should affect a person from within so that it may progressively enlighten him and render him continually more like Christ.

b) Confession

The sacrament of penance includes the confession of sins, which comes from true knowledge of self before God and from contrition for those sins. However, this inner examination of heart and the exterior accusation should be made in the light of God's mercy. Confession requires in the penitent the desire to open his heart to the minister of God, and in the minister a spiritual judgment by which, acting in the person of Christ, he pronounces his decision of forgiveness or retention of sins in accord with the power of the keys.[32]

169

c) Act of Penance (Satisfaction)

True conversion is completed by acts of penance or satisfaction for sins committed, by amendment of conduct, and also by the reparation of injury.[33] The kind and extent of the satisfaction should be suited to the personal condition of each penitent so that each one may restore the order which he disturbed and through the corresponding remedy be cured of the sickness from which he suffered. Therefore, it is necessary that the act of penance really be a remedy for sin and a help to renewal of life. Thus the penitent, "forgetting the things which are behind him" (Philippians 3:13), again becomes part of the mystery of salvation and turns himself toward the future.

d) Absolution

Through the sign of absolution God grants pardon to the sinner who in sacramental confession manifests his change of heart to the Church's minister, and thus the sacrament of penance is completed. In God's design the humanity and loving kindness of our Savior have visibly appeared to us,[34] and God uses visible signs to give salvation and to renew the broken covenant.

In the sacrament of penance the Father receives the repentant son who comes back to him, Christ places the lost sheep on his shoulders and brings it back to the sheepfold, and the Holy Spirit sanctifies this temple of God again or lives more fully within it. This is finally expressed in a renewed and more fervent sharing of the Lord's table, and there is great joy at the banquet of God's Church over the son who has returned from afar.[35]

The Necessity and Benefit of the Sacrament

7. Just as the wound of sin is varied and multiple in the life of individuals and of the community, so too the healing which penance provides is varied. Those who by grave sin have withdrawn from the communion of love with God are called back in the sacrament of penance to the life they had lost. And those who through daily weakness fall into venial sins draw strength from a repeated celebration of penance to gain the full freedom of the children of God.

a) To obtain the saving remedy of the sacrament of penance, according to the plan of our merciful God, the faithful must confess to a priest each and every grave sin which they remember upon examination of conscience.[36]

b) Moreover, frequent and careful celebration of this sacrament is also very useful as a remedy for venial sins. This is not a mere ritual repetition or psychological exercise, but a serious striving to perfect the grace of baptism so that, as we bear in our body the death of Jesus Christ, his life may be seen in us ever more clearly.[37] In confession of this kind, penitents who accuse themselves of venial faults should try to conform more closely to Christ and to follow the voice of the Spirit more attentively.

In order that this sacrament of healing may truly achieve its purpose among Christ's faithful, it must take root in their whole lives and move them to more fervent service of God and neighbor.

The celebration of this sacrament is thus always an act in which the Church proclaims its faith, gives thanks to God for the freedom with which Christ has made us free,[38] and offers its life as a spiritual sacrifice in praise of God's glory, as it hastens to meet the Lord Jesus.

III. OFFICES AND MINISTRIES IN THE RECONCILIATION OF PENITENTS

The Community in the Celebration of Penance

8. The whole Church, as a priestly people, acts in different ways in the work of reconciliation which has been entrusted to it by the Lord. Not only does the Church call sinners to repentance by preaching the word of God, but it also intercedes for them and helps penitents with maternal care and solicitude to acknowledge and admit their sins and so to obtain the mercy of God who alone can forgive sins. Furthermore, the Church becomes the instrument of the conversion and absolution of the penitent through the ministry entrusted by Christ to the apostles and their successors.[39]

9. *The Minister of the Sacrament of Penance*

a) The Church exercises the ministry of the sacrament of penance through bishops and presbyters. By preaching God's word they call the faithful to conversion; in the name of Christ and by the power of the Holy Spirit they declare and grant the forgiveness of sins.

In the exercise of this ministry presbyters act in communion with the bishop and share in his power and office of regulating the penitential discipline.[40]

b) The competent minister of the sacrament of penance is a priest who has the faculty to absolve in accordance with canon law. All priests, however, even though not approved to hear confessions, absolve validly and licitly all penitents who are in danger of death.

10. *The Pastoral Exercise of This Ministry*

a) In order to fulfill his ministry properly and faithfully the confessor should understand the disorders of souls and apply the appropriate remedies to them. He should fulfill his office of judge wisely and should acquire the knowledge and prudence necessary for this task by serious study, guided by the teaching authority of the Church and especially by fervent prayer to God. Discernment of spirits is a deep knowledge of God's action in the hearts of men; it is a gift of the Spirit as well as the fruit of charity.[41]

b) The confessor should always be ready and willing to hear the confessions of the faithful whenever they make a reasonable request of him.[42]

c) By receiving the repentant sinner and leading him to the light of truth the confessor fulfills a paternal function: he reveals the heart of the Father and shows the image of Christ the Good Shepherd. He should keep in mind that he has been entrusted with the ministry of Christ, who mercifully accomplished the saving work of man's redemption and who is present by his power in the sacraments.[43]

d) As the minister of God the confessor comes to know the secrets of another's conscience, and he is bound to keep the sacramental seal of confession absolutely inviolate.

The Penitent

11. The acts of the penitent in the celebration of the sacrament are of the greatest importance.

When with proper dispositions he approaches this saving remedy instituted by Christ and confesses his sins, he shares by his actions in the sacrament itself; the sacrament is completed when the words of absolution are spoken by the minister in the name of Christ.

Thus the faithful Christian, as he experiences and proclaims the mercy of God in his life, celebrates with the priest the liturgy by which the Church continually renews itself.

IV. THE CELEBRATION OF THE SACRAMENT OF PENANCE

The Place of Celebration

12. The sacrament of penance is celebrated in the place and location prescribed by law.

The Time of Celebration

13. The reconciliation of penitents may be celebrated at any time on any day, but it is desirable that the faithful know the day and time at which the priest is available for this ministry. They should be encouraged to approach the sacrament of penance at the times when Mass is not being celebrated and especially during the scheduled periods.[44]

The season of Lent is most appropriate for celebrating the sacrament of penance. Already on Ash Wednesday the people of God has heard the solemn invitation: "Turn away from sin and believe the good news." It is therefore fitting to have several penitential celebrations during Lent, so that all the faithful may have an opportunity to be reconciled with God and their neighbor and so be able to celebrate the paschal mystery in the Easter triduum with renewed hearts.

Liturgical Vestments

14. The regulations laid down by the local Ordinaries for the use of liturgical vestments in the celebration of penance are to be observed.

A

RITE FOR THE RECONCILIATION OF INDIVIDUAL PENITENTS

Preparation of Priest and Penitent

15. Priest and penitent should first prepare themselves by prayer to celebrate the sacrament. The priest should call upon the Holy Spirit so that he may receive enlightenment and charity. The penitent should compare his life with the example and commandments of Christ and then pray to God for the forgiveness of his sins.

Welcoming the Penitent

16. The priest should welcome the penitent with fraternal charity and, if the occasion permits, address him with friendly words. The penitent then makes the sign of the cross, saying: "In the name of the Father, and of the Son, and of the Holy Spirit. Amen." The priest may also make the sign of the cross with the penitent. Next the priest briefly urges the penitent to have confidence in God. If the penitent is unknown to the priest, it is proper for him to indicate his state in life, the time of his last confession, his difficulties in leading the Christian life, and anything else which may help the confessor in exercising his ministry.

Reading the Word of God

17. Then the priest, or the penitent himself may read a text of holy Scripture, or this may be done as part of the preparation for the sacrament. Through the word of God the Christian receives light to recognize his sins and is called to conversion and to confidence in God's mercy.

Confession of Sins and the Act of Penance

18. The penitent then confesses his sins, beginning, where customary, with a form of general confession: I confess to almighty God. If necessary, the priest should help the penitent to make a complete confession; he should also encourage him to have sincere sorrow for his sins against God. Finally, the priest should offer suitable counsel to help the penitent begin a new life and, where necessary, instruct him in the duties of the Christian way of life.

If the penitent has been the cause of harm or scandal to others, the priest should lead him to resolve that he will make appropriate restitution.

Then the priest imposes an act of penance or satisfaction on the penitent; this should serve not only to make up for the past but also help him to begin a new life and provide him with an antidote to weakness. As far as possible, the penance should correspond to the seriousness and nature of the sins. This act of penance may suitably take the form of prayer, self-denial, and especially service of one's neighbor and works of mercy. These will underline the fact that sin and its forgiveness bear a social aspect.

The Prayer of the Penitent and the Absolution by the Priest

19. After this the penitent manifests his contrition and resolution to begin a new life by means of a prayer for God's pardon. It is desirable that this prayer should be based on the words of Scripture.

Following this prayer, the priest extends his hands, or at least his right hand, over the head of the penitent and pronounces the formula of absolution, in which the essential words are: "I absolve you from your sins in the name of the Father and of the Son and of the Holy Spirit." As he says the words the priest makes the sign of the cross over the penitent. The form of absolution (see no. 46) indicates that the reconciliation of the penitent comes from the mercy of the Father; it shows the connection between the reconciliation of the sinner and the paschal mystery of Christ; it stresses the role of the Holy Spirit in the forgiveness of sins; finally, it underlines the ecclesial aspect of the sacrament because reconciliation with God is asked for and given through the ministry of the Church.

Proclamation of Praise and Dismissal of the Penitent

20. After receiving pardon for his sins the penitent praises the mercy of God and gives him thanks in a short invocation taken from scripture. Then the priest tells him to go in peace.

The penitent continues his conversion and expresses it by a life renewed according to the Gospel and more and more steeped in the love of God, for "love covers over a multitude of sins" (1 Peter 4:8).

21. When pastoral need dictates it, the priest may omit or shorten some parts of the rite but must always retain in their entirety the confession of sins and the acceptance of the act of penance, the invitation (no. 44), and the form of absolution and the dismissal. In imminent danger of death, it is sufficient for the priest to say the essential words of the form of absolution, namely, "I absolve you from your sins in the name of the Father, and of the Son, and of the Holy Spirit."

B

RITE FOR RECONCILIATION OF SEVERAL PENITENTS WITH INDIVIDUAL CONFESSION AND ABSOLUTION

22. When a number of penitents assemble at the same time to receive sacramental reconciliation, it is fitting that they be prepared for the sacrament by a celebration of the word of God.

Those who will receive the sacrament at another time may also take part in the service.

Communal celebration shows more clearly the ecclesial nature of penance. The faithful listen together to the word of God, which proclaims his mercy and invites them to conversion; at the same time they examine the conformity of their lives with that word of God and help each other through common prayer. After each person has confessed his sins and received absolution, all praise God together for his wonderful deeds on behalf of the people he has gained for himself through the blood of his Son.

If necessary, several priests should be available in suitable places to hear individual confessions and to reconcile the penitents.

Introductory Rites

23. When the faithful are assembled, a suitable hymn may be sung. Then the priest greets them, and, if necessary, he or another minister gives a brief introduction to the celebration and explains the order of service. Next he invites all to pray and after a period of silence completes the (opening) prayer.

The Celebration of the Word of God

24. The sacrament of penance should begin with a hearing of God's word, because through his word God calls men to repentance and leads them to a true conversion of heart.

One or more readings may be chosen. If more than one are read, a psalm, another suitable song or a period of silence should be inserted between them, so that the word of God may be more deeply understood and heartfelt assent may be given to it. If there is only one reading, it is preferable that it be from the gospel.

Readings should be chosen which illustrate the following:

a) the voice of God calling men back to conversion and ever closer conformity with Christ;

b) the mystery of our reconciliation through the death and resurrection of Christ and through the gift of the Holy Spirit;

c) the judgment of God about good and evil in men's lives as a help in the examination of conscience.

25. The homily, taking its theme from the scriptural text, should lead the penitents to examine their consciences and to turn away from sin and towards God. It should remind the faithful that sin works against God, against the community and one's neigh-

bors, and against the sinner himself. Therefore, it would be good to recall:

a) the infinite mercy of God, greater than all our sins, by which again and again he calls us back to himself;

b) the need for interior repentance, by which we are genuinely prepared to make reparation for sin;

c) the social aspect of grace and sin, by which the actions of individuals in some degree affect the whole body of the Church;

d) the duty to make satisfaction for sin, which is effective because of Christ's work of reparation and requires especially, in addition to works of penance, the exercise of true charity toward God and neighbor.

26. After the homily a suitable period of silence should be allowed for examining one's conscience and awakening true contrition for sin. The priest or a deacon or other minister may help the faithful with brief considerations or a litany, adapted to their background, age, etc.

If it is judged suitable, this communal examination of conscience and awakening of contrition may take the place of the homily. But in this case it should be clearly based on the text of scripture that has just been read.

The Rite of Reconciliation

27. At the invitation of the deacon or other minister, all kneel or bow their heads and say a form of general confession (for example, *I confess to almighty God*). Then they stand and join in a litany or suitable song to express confession of sins, heartfelt contrition, prayer for forgiveness, and trust in God's mercy. Finally, they say the Lord's Prayer, which is never omitted.

28. After the Lord's Prayer the priests go to the places assigned for confession. The penitents who desire to confess their sins go to the priest of their choice. After receiving a suitable act of penance, they are absolved by him with the form for the reconciliation of an individual penitent.

29. When the confessions are over, the priests return to the sanctuary. The priest who presides invites all to make an act of thanksgiving and to praise God for his mercy. This may be done in a psalm or hymn or litany. Finally, the priest concludes the celebration with prayer, praising God for the great love he has shown us.

Dismissal of the People

30. After the prayer of thanksgiving the priest blesses the faithful. Then the deacon or the priest himself dismisses the congregation.

C

RITE FOR RECONCILIATION OF PENITENTS WITH GENERAL CONFESSION AND ABSOLUTION

The Discipline of General Absolution

31. Individual, integral confession and absolution remain the only ordinary way for the faithful to reconcile themselves with God and the Church, unless physical or moral impossibility excuses from this kind of confession.

Particular, occasional circumstances may render it lawful and even necessary to give general absolution to a number of penitents without their previous individual confession.

In addition to cases involving danger of death, it is

lawful to give sacramental absolution to several of the faithful at the same time, after they have made only a generic confession but have been suitably called to repentance, if there is grave need, namely when, in view of the number of penitents, sufficient confessors are not available to hear individual confessions properly within a suitable period of time, so that the penitents would, through no fault of their own, have to go without sacramental grace or holy communion for a long time. This may happen especially in mission territories but in other places as well and also in groups of persons when the need is established.

General absolution is not lawful when confessors are available, for the sole reason of the large number of penitents, as may be on the occasion of some major feast or pilgrimage.[45]

32. The judgment about the presence of the above conditions and the decision concerning the lawfulness of giving general sacramental absolution are reserved to the bishop of the diocese, who is to consult with the other members of the episcopal conference.

Over and above the cases determined by the diocesan bishop, if any other serious need arises for giving sacramental absolution to several persons together, the priest must have recourse to the local Ordinary beforehand, when this is possible, if he is to give absolution lawfully. Otherwise, he should inform the Ordinary as soon as possible of the need and of the absolution which he gave.[46]

33. In order that the faithful may profit from sacramental absolution given to several persons at the same time, it is absolutely necessary that they be properly disposed. Each one should be sorry for his sins and resolve to avoid committing them again. He should intend to repair any scandal and harm he may have caused and likewise resolve to confess in due

time each one of the grave sins which he cannot confess at present. These dispositions and conditions, which are required for the validity of the sacrament, should be carefully recalled to the faithful by priests.[47]

34. Those who receive pardon for grave sins by a common absolution should go to individual confession before they receive this kind of absolution again, unless they are impeded by a just reason. They are strictly bound, unless this is morally impossible, to go to confession within a year. The precept which obliges each of the faithful to confess at least once a year to a priest all the grave sins which he has not individually confessed before also remains in force in this case too.[48]

The Rite of General Absolution

35. For the reconciliation of penitents by general confession and absolution in the cases provided by law, everything takes place as described above for the reconciliation of several penitents with individual confession and absolution, with the following exceptions:

a) After the homily or during it, the faithful who seek general absolution should be instructed to dispose themselves properly, that is, each one should be sorry for his sins and resolve to avoid committing them again. He should intend to repair any scandal and harm he may have caused and likewise resolve to confess in due time each one of the grave sins which cannot be confessed at present.[49] Some act of penance should be proposed for all; individuals may add to this penance if they wish.

b) The deacon, another minister, or the priest then calls upon the penitents who wish to receive absolution to show their intention by some sign (for example, by bowing their heads, kneeling, or giving some other sign determined by the episcopal conferences). They should also say together a form of general confession (for example, *I confess to almighty God*), which may be followed by a litany or a penitential song. Then the Lord's Prayer is sung or said by all, as indicated in no. 27 above.

c) Then the priest calls upon the grace of the Holy Spirit for the forgiveness of sins, proclaims the victory over sin of Christ's death and resurrection, and gives sacramental absolution to the penitents.

d) Finally, the priest invites the people to give thanks, described in no. 29, above, and, omitting the concluding prayer, he immediately blesses and dismisses them.

V. PENITENTIAL CELEBRATIONS

Nature and Structure

36. Penitential celebrations are gatherings of the people of God to hear the proclamation of God's word. This invites them to conversion and renewal of life and announces our freedom from sin through the death and resurrection of Christ. The structure of these services is the same as that usually followed in celebrations of the word of God[50] and is given in the *Rite for Reconciliation of Several Penitents.*

It is appropriate, therefore, that after the introductory rites (song, greeting, and prayer) one or more biblical readings be chosen with songs, psalms, or periods of silence inserted between them. In the homily these readings should be explained and applied to the congregation. Before or after the readings from scripture, readings from the Fathers or other writers may be selected which will help the community and each person to a true awareness of sin and heartfelt sorrow, in other words, to bring about conversion of life.

After the homily and reflection on God's word, it is desirable that the congregation, united in voice and spirit, pray together in a litany or in some other way suited to general participation. At the end the Lord's Prayer is said, asking God our Father "to forgive us our sins as we forgive those who sin against us . . . and deliver us from evil." The priest or the minister who presides concludes with a prayer and the dismissal of the people.

Benefit and Importance

37. Care should be taken that the faithful do not confuse these celebrations with the celebration of the sacrament of penance.[51] Penitential celebrations are very helpful in promoting conversion of life and purification of heart.[52]

It is desirable to arrange such services especially for these purposes:

—to foster the spirit of penance within the Christian community;

—to help the faithful to prepare for confession which can be made individually later at a convenient time;

—to help children gradually to form their conscience about sin in human life and freedom from sin through Christ;

—to help catechumens during their conversion.

Penitential celebrations, moreover, are very useful in places where no priest is available to give sacramental absolution. They offer help in reaching that perfect contrition which comes from charity and enables the faithful to attain to God's grace through a desire for the sacrament of penance.[53]

VI.   ADAPTATIONS OF THE RITE TO DIFFERENT REGIONS AND CIRCUMSTANCES

Adaptations by the Episcopal Conferences

38. In preparing particular rituals episcopal conferences may adapt this rite of penance to the needs of individual regions so that after confirmation by the Apostolic See the rituals may be used in the respective regions. It is the responsibility of episcopal conferences in this matter:

a) to establish regulations for the discipline of the sacrament of penance, particularly those affecting the ministry of the priests and the reservation of sins;

b) to determine more precise regulations about the place proper for the ordinary celebration of the sacrament of penance and about the signs of penance to be shown by the faithful before general absolution (see no. 35, above);

c) to prepare translations of texts adapted to the character and language of each people and also to compose new texts for the prayers of the faithful and the minister, keeping intact the sacramental form.

The Competence of the Bishop

39. It is for the diocesan bishop:

a) to regulate the discipline of penance in his diocese,[54] including adaptations of the rite according to the rules proposed by the episcopal conference;

b) to determine, after consultation with the other members of the episcopal conference, when general sacramental absolution may be permitted under the conditions established by the Holy See.[55]

Adaptations by the Minister

40. It is for priests, and especially parish priests:

a) in reconciling individuals or the community, to adapt the rite to the concrete circumstances of the penitents. The essential structure and the entire form of absolution must be kept, but if necessary they may omit some parts for pastoral reasons or enlarge upon them, may select the texts of readings or prayers, and may choose a place more suitable for the celebration according to the regulations of the episcopal conference, so that the entire celebration may be rich and fruitful;

b) to propose and prepare occasional penitential celebrations during the year, especially in Lent. In order that the texts chosen and the order of the celebration may be adapted to the conditions and circumstances of the community or group (for example, children, sick persons, etc.), they may be assisted by others, including the laity;

c) to decide to give general sacramental absolution preceded by only a generic confession, when a grave necessity not foreseen by the diocesan bishop arises and when recourse to him is not possible. They are obliged to notify the Ordinary as soon as possible of the need and of the fact that absolution was given.

NOTES

1. See 2 Corinthians 5:18ff; Colossians 1:20.
2. See John 8:34-36.
3. See 1 Peter 2:9.
4. See Luke 15.
5. Luke 5:20, 27-32; 7:48.
6. See Matthew 9:2-8.
7. See Romans 4:25.
8. See Roman Missal, Eucharistic Prayer III.
9. See Matthew 26:28.
10. See John 20:19-23.
11. See Luke 24:47.
12. See Acts 3:19, 26; 17:30.
13. See Romans 6:4-10.
14. Roman Missal, Eucharistic Prayer III.
15. Roman Missal, Eucharistic Prayer II.
16. See Council of Trent, Session XIV, De sacramento
Paenitentiae, Chapter 1: Denz.-Schon. 1668 and 1670; can. 1:
Denz.-Schon. 1701.
17. St. Ambrose, Letter 41:12: *PL* 16, 1116.
18. See Revelation 19:7.
19. See Ephesians 1:22-23; Second Vatican Council, constitution *Lumen gentium,* no. 7: *AAS* 57 (1965) 9-11.
20. Second Vatican Council, constitution *Lumen gentium,*
no. 8: *ibid.,* 12.
21. See 1 Peter 4:13.
22. See 1 Peter 4:8.
23. See Council of Trent, Session XIV, De sacramento
Paenitentiae: Denz.-Schon. 1638, 1740, 1743; Congregation of
Rites, instruction *Eucharisticum mysterium,* May 25, 1967,
no. 35: *AAS* 59 (1967) 560-561; Roman Missal, *General Instruction,* nos. 29, 30, 56 a. b. g.
24. Second Vatican Council, constitution *Lumen gentium,*
no. 11: *AAS* 57 (1965) 15-16.
25. Paul VI, Apostolic Constitution *Paenitemini,* February 17,
1966: *AAS* 58 (1966) 179; See Second Vatican Council, constitution *Lumen gentium,* no. 11: *AAS* 57 (1965) 15-16.
26. See Galatians 2:20; Ephesians 5:25.
27. See Titus 3:6.
28. Paul VI, Apostolic Constitution *Indulgentiarum doctrina,*
January 1, 1967, no. 4: *AAS* 59 (1967) 9; see Pius XII,
encyclical *Mystici Corporis,* June 29, 1943: *AAS* 35 (1943) 213.

29. See Council of Trent, Session XIV, De sacramento Paenitentiae, Chapter 1: Denz.-Schon. 1673-1675.
30. *Ibid.,* Chapter 4: Denz.-Schon. 1676.
31. Paul VI, Apostolic Constitution *Paenitemini,* February 17, 1966: *AAS* 58 (1966) 179.
32. See Council of Trent, Session XIV, De sacramento Paenitentiae, Chapter 5: Denz.-Schon. 1679.
33. See Council of Trent, Session XIV, De sacramento Paenitentiae, Chapter 8: Denz.-Schon. 1690-1692; Paul VI, Apostolic Constitution *Indulgentiarum doctrina,* January 1, 1967, nos. 2-3: *AAS* 59 (1967) 6-8.
34. See Titus 3:4-5.
35. See Luke 15:7, 10, 32.
36. See Council of Trent, Session XIV, De sacramento Paenitentiae, can. 7-8: Denz.-Schon. 1707-1708.
37. See 2 Corinthians 4:10.
38. See Galatians 4:31.
39. See Matthew 18:18; John 20:23.
40. See Second Vatican Council, constitution *Lumen gentium,* no. 26: *AAS* 57 (1965) 31-32.
41. See Philippians 1:9-10.
42. See Congregation for the Doctrine of the Faith, *Normae pastorales circa absolutionem sacramentalem generali modo impertiendam,* June 16, 1972, No. XII: *AAS* 64 (1972) 514.
43. See Second Vatican Council, constitution *Sacrosanctum Concilium,* no. 7: *AAS* 56 (1964) 100-101.
44. See Congregation of Rites, instruction *Eucharisticum mysterium,* May 25, 1967, no. 35: *AAS* 59 (1967) 560-561.
45. Congregation for the Doctrine of the Faith, *Normae pastorales circa absolutionem sacramentalem generali modo impertiendam,* June 16, 1972, no. III: *AAS* 64 (1972) 511.
46. *Ibid.;* no. V: *loc. cit.,* 512.
47. *Ibid.,* nos. VI and XI: *loc. cit.,* 512, 514.
48. *Ibid.,* nos. VII and VIII: *loc. cit.,* 512-513.
49. See *ibid.,* no. VI: *loc. cit.,* 512.
50. See Congregation of Rites, instruction *Inter Oecumenici,* September 26, 1964, nos. 37-39: *AAS* 56 (1964) 110-111.
51. See Congregation for the Doctrine of the Faith, *Normae pastorales circa absolutionem sacramentalem generali modo impertiendam,* June 16, 1972, no. X: *AAS* 64 (1972) 513-514.
52. *Ibid.*
53. See Council of Trent, Session XIV, De sacramento Paenitentiae, chapter 5: Denz.-Schon. 1677.
54. See Second Vatican Council, constitution *Lumen gentium,* no. 26: *AAS* 57 (1965) 31-32.
55. See Congregation for the Doctrine of the Faith, *Normae pastorales circa absolutionem sacramentalem generali modo impertiendam,* no. V: *AAS* 64 (1972) 512.

189

Chapter I

RITE FOR RECONCILIATION OF INDIVIDUAL PENITENTS

(See pages 61-72)

Chapter II

RITE FOR RECONCILIATION OF SEVERAL PENITENTS WITH INDIVIDUAL CONFESSION AND ABSOLUTION

Introductory Rites

48.   *Song*

When the faithful have assembled, they may sing a psalm, antiphon, or other appropriate song while the priest is entering the church, for example:

Hear us, Lord,
for you are merciful and kind.
In your great compassion,
look on us with love.

Or:

Let us come with confidence before the throne of
    grace to receive God's mercy,
and we shall find pardon and strength
in our time of need.

190

49. *Greeting*

After the song the priest greets the congregation:

Grace, mercy, and peace be with you
from God the Father
and Christ Jesus our Savior.

R.   And also with you.

Or:

Grace and peace be with you
from God the Father
and from Jesus Christ
who loved us
and washed away our sins in his blood.

R.   Glory to him for ever. Amen.

Or:

Grace, mercy, and peace   [94]
from God the Father and Jesus Christ his Son
be with you in truth and love.

R.   Amen.

Or:

May God open your hearts to his law   [95]
and give you peace;
may he answer your prayers
and restore you to friendship.

R.   Amen.

Or:

Grace and peace be with you   [96]

from God our Father
and from the Lord Jesus Christ
who laid down his life for our sins.

R.   Glory to him for ever. Amen.

*Then the priest or another minister speaks briefly
about the importance and purpose of the celebration
and the order of the service.*

50.   *Opening Prayer*

The priest invites all to pray, using these or similar words:

Brothers and sisters, God calls us to conversion; let us therefore ask him for the grace of sincere repentance.

All pray in silence for a brief period. Then the priest sings or says the prayer:

Lord,
hear the prayers of those who call on you,
forgive the sins of those who confess to you,
and in your merciful love
give us your pardon and your peace.

We ask this through Christ our Lord.

R.   Amen.

Or:

Lord,
send your Spirit among us
to cleanse us in the waters of repentance.
May he make of us a living sacrifice
so that in every place,
by his life-giving power,

we may praise your glory
and proclaim your loving compassion.

We ask this through Christ our Lord.

R.   Amen.

Or:

Lord,   [97]
turn to us in mercy
and forgive us all our sins
that we may serve you in true freedom.

We ask this through Christ our Lord.

R.   Amen.

Or:

Lord our God,   [98]
you are patient with sinners
and accept our desire to make amends.
We acknowledge our sins
and are resolved to change our lives.
Help us to celebrate this sacrament of your mercy
so that we may reform our lives
and receive from you the gift of everlasting joy.

We ask this through Christ our Lord.

R.   Amen.

Or:

Almighty and merciful God,   [99]
you have brought us together in the name of your Son
to receive your mercy and grace in our time of need.
Open our eyes to see the evil we have done.
Touch our hearts and convert us to yourself.

Where sin has divided and scattered,
may your love make one again;
where sin has brought weakness,
may your power heal and strengthen;
where sin has brought death,
may your Spirit raise to new life.

Give us a new heart to love you,
so that our lives may reflect the image of your Son.
May the world see the glory of Christ
revealed in your Church,
and come to know
that he is the one whom you have sent,
Jesus Christ, your Son, our Lord.

R.   Amen.

Or:

Father of mercies   [100]
and God of all consolation,
you do not wish the sinner to die
but to be converted and live.
Come to the aid of your people,
that they may turn from their sins
and live for you alone.
May we be attentive to your word,
confess our sins, receive your forgiveness,
and be always grateful for your loving kindness.
Help us to live the truth in love
and grow into the fullness of Christ, your Son,
who lives and reigns for ever and ever.

R.   **Amen.**

Celebration of the Word of God

51.   *The celebration of the word follows. If there are*

194

several readings a psalm or other appropriate song or even a period of silence should intervene between them, so that everyone may understand the word of God more deeply and give it his heartfelt assent. If there is only one reading, it is preferable that it be from the gospel.

First Example

Love is the fullness of the law

First Reading (Deuteronomy 5:1-3, 6-7, 11-12, 16-21a; 6:4-6)
> Love the Lord your God with all your heart.

Responsorial Psalm (Baruch 1:15-22)
> R. (3, 2) Listen and have pity, Lord, because you are merciful.

Second Reading (Ephesians 5:1-14)
> Walk in love, as Christ loved us.

Gospel Acclamation (John 8:12)
> I am the light of the world.
> The man who follows me will have the light of life.

Gospel (Matthew 22:34-40)
> On these two commandments
> the whole law and the prophets depend.

Or: (John 13:34-35; 15: 10-13)
> I give you a new commandment:
> love one another.

Second Example

> Your mind must be renewed.

First Reading (Isaiah 1:10-18)
   Stop doing what is wrong, and learn to do good.

Responsorial Psalm (Psalm 50, especially verses 18-19)
   R.   *(19a)*   A humbled heart is pleasing to God.

Second Reading (Ephesians 4:23-32)
   Your mind must be renewed by a spiritual revo-
   lution.

Gospel Acclamation (Matthew 11:28)
   Come to me, all you who labor and are bur-
      dened,
   and I will give you rest.

Gospel (Matthew 5: 1-12)
   Happy are the poor in spirit.

Other optional texts are given in nos. 101-201.

52.   Homily

   *The homily which follows is based on the texts
of the readings and should lead the penitents to examine their consciences and renew their lives.*

53.   Examination of Conscience

   *A period of time may be spent in making
an examination of conscience and in arousing true
sorrow for sins. The priest, deacon, or another minister
may help the faithful by brief statements or a kind of
litany, taking into consideration their circumstances,
age, etc.*

Rite of Reconciliation

54.   General Confession of Sins

   The deacon or another minister invites all to

kneel or bow, and to join in saying a general formula for confession (for example, I confess to almighty God). Then they stand and say a litany or sing an appropriate song. The Lord's Prayer is always added at the end.

First Example

Deacon or minister:

My brothers and sisters, confess your sins and pray for each other, that you may be healed.

All say:

I confess to almighty God,
and to you, my brothers and sisters,
that I have sinned through my own fault

> *They strike their breast:*

in my thoughts and in my words,
in what I have done,
and in what I have failed to do;
and I ask blessed Mary, ever virgin,
all the angels and saints,
and you, my brothers and sisters,
to pray for me to the Lord our God.

Deacon or minister:

The Lord is merciful. He makes us clean of heart and leads us out into his freedom when we acknowledge our guilt. Let us ask him to forgive us and bind up the wounds inflicted by our sins.

Give us the grace of true repentance.
R.   We pray you, hear us.

Pardon your servants and release them from the debt

of sin.
R.   We pray you, hear us.

Forgive your children who confess their sins, and re-
     store them to full communion with your Church.
R.   We pray you, hear us.

Renew the glory of baptism in those who have lost it
     by sin.
R.   We pray you, hear us.

Welcome them to your altar, and renew their spirit
     with the hope of eternal glory.
R.   We pray you, hear us.

Keep them faithful to your sacraments and loyal in
     your service.
R.   We pray you, hear us.

Renew the love in their hearts, and make them bear
     witness to it in their daily lives.
R.   We pray you, hear us.

Keep them always obedient to your commandments
     and protect within them your gift of eternal life.
R.   We pray you, hear us.

Deacon or minister:

Let us now pray to God our Father in the words Christ
gave us, and ask him for his forgiveness and protection
from all evil.

  All say together:

Our Father . . .

  The priest concludes:

Lord,
draw near to your servants
who in the presence of your Church
confess that they are sinners.
Through the ministry of the Church
free them from all sin
so that renewed in spirit
they may give you thankful praise.

We ask this through Christ our Lord.
R.   Amen.

Second Example

Deacon or minister:

Brothers and sisters, let us call to mind the goodness of God our Father, and acknowledge our sins, so that we may receive his merciful forgiveness.

All say:

I confess to almighty God,
and to you, my brothers and sisters,
that I have sinned through my own fault

They strike their breast:

in my thoughts and in my words,
in what I have done,
and in what I have failed to do;
and I ask blessed Mary, ever virgin,
all the angels and saints,
and you, my brothers and sisters,
to pray for me to the Lord our God.

Deacon or minister:

Christ our Savior is our advocate with the Father: with humble hearts let us ask him to forgive us our sins and cleanse us from every stain.

You were sent with good news for the poor and healing for the contrite.
R.   Lord, be merciful to me, a sinner.

Or:

Lord, have mercy.

You came to call sinners, not the just.
R.   Lord, be merciful to me, a sinner.

Or:

Lord, have mercy.

You forgave the many sins of the woman who showed you great love.
R.   Lord, be merciful to me, a sinner.

Or:

Lord, have mercy.

You did not shun the company of outcasts and sinners.
R.   Lord, be merciful to me, a sinner.

Or:

Lord, have mercy.

You carried back to the fold the sheep that had strayed.
R.   Lord, be merciful to me, a sinner.

Or:

Lord, have mercy.

You did not condemn the woman taken in adultery,
but sent her away in peace.

R.   Lord, be merciful to me, a sinner.

Or:

Lord, have mercy.

You called Zacchaeus to repentance and a new life.

R.   Lord, be merciful to me, a sinner.

Or:

Lord, have mercy.

You promised Paradise to the repentant thief.

R.   Lord, be merciful to me, a sinner.

Or:

Lord, have mercy.

You are always interceding for us at the right hand of
the Father.

R.   Lord, be merciful to me, a sinner.

Or:

Lord, have mercy.

Deacon or minister:

Now, in obedience to Christ himself, let us join in
prayer to the Father, asking him to forgive us as we
forgive others.

All say together:

Our Father . . .

The priest concludes:

Father, our source of life,
you know our weakness.
May we reach out with joy to grasp your hand
and walk more readily in your ways.

We ask this through Christ our Lord.

R.   Amen.

Or:

[202]

If the prayer is directed to the Father:

1

Dear friends in Christ, our merciful Father does not
desire the death of the sinner but rather that he should
turn back to him and have life. Let us pray that we who
are sorry for our past sins may fear no future evil and
sin no more.

R.   Spare us, Lord; spare your people.

2

God who is infinitely merciful pardons all who are repentant and takes away their guilt. Confident in his
goodness, let us ask him to forgive all our sins as we
confess them with sincerity of heart.

R.   Lord, hear our prayer.

God gave us his Son for our sins and raised him up to make us holy. Let us humbly pray to the Father.

R.   Lord, have mercy on your people.

God our Father waits for the return of those who are lost and welcomes them back as his children. Let us pray that we may turn back to him and be received with kindness into his house.

R.   Lord, do not hold our sins against us.

Or:

Father, we have sinned in your sight; we are unworthy to be called your children.

Our God seeks out what is lost, leads home the abandoned, binds up what is broken and gives strength to the weak; let us ask him to help us.

R.   Lord, heal our weakness.

Or:

If the prayer is directed to Christ: [203]

Jesus Christ is the victor over sin and death: in his mercy may he pardon our offenses against God and reconcile us with the Church we have wounded by our sins.

R.   Lord Jesus, be our salvation.

2

In his great love Christ willingly suffered and died for our sins and for the sins of all mankind. Let us come before him with faith and hope to pray for the salvation of the world.

R.   Christ, graciously hear us.

3

Let us pray with confidence to Christ, the Good Shepherd, who seeks out the lost sheep and carries it back with joy.

R.   Lord, seek us out and bring us home.

4

Christ our Lord bore our sins upon the cross and by his suffering has brought us healing, so that we live for God and are dead to sin. Let us pray with humility and trust.

R.   Lord, to whom shall we go? You have the words of eternal life. We have come to believe and to know that you are the Christ, the Son of God.

Or:

Have pity on us, and help us.

5

Christ our Lord was given up to death for our sins and rose again for our justification. Let us pray to him with confidence in his goodness.

R.   You are our Savior.

Or:

Jesus Christ, Son of the living God, have pity on us.

Or: [204]

(At least one of the intercessions should always be a petition for a true conversion of heart.)

If the prayer is addressed to the Father:

1

—By human weakness we have disfigured the holiness of the Church: pardon all our sins and restore us to full communion with our brethren.

R. Lord, hear our prayer. *Or:* Lord, hear us.

Or another suitable response may be used.

—Your mercy is our hope: welcome us to the sacrament of reconciliation. R.

—Give us the will to change our lives, and the lives of others, by charity, good example and prayer. R.

—As we make our confession, rescue us from slavery to sin and lead us to the freedom enjoyed by your children. R.

—Make us a living sign of your love for all to see: people reconciled with you and with each other. R.

—Through the sacrament of reconciliation may we grow in your peace and seek to spread it throughout the world. R.

—In this sign of your love you forgive us our sins: may it teach us to love others and to forgive their sins against us.   R.

—In your mercy clothe us in the wedding garment of grace and welcome us to your table.   R.

—Forgive us our sins, lead us in the ways of goodness and love, and bring us to the reward of everlasting peace.   R.

—Give light to our darkness and lead us by your truth.   R.

—In justice you punish us: in your mercy set us free for the glory of your name.   R.

—May your power keep safe from all danger those whom your love sets free from the chains of sin.   R.

—Look on our weakness: do not be angry and condemn, but in your love cleanse, guide and save us.   R.

—In your mercy free us from the past and enable us to begin a new life of holiness.   R.

—When we stray from you, guide us back into the way of holiness, love and peace.   R.

—By your redeeming love overcome our sinfulness and the harm it has brought us.   R.

—Blot out the sins of the past and fit us for the life that is to come.   R.

2

The following intercessions may be used with a variable response or with an invariable response as in the Liturgy of the Hours.

In your goodness forgive our sins against the unity of your family,
—make us one in heart, one in spirit.

We have sinned, Lord, we have sinned,
—take away our sins by your saving grace.

Give us pardon for our sins,
—and reconciliation with your Church.

Touch our hearts and change our lives, make us grow always in your friendship,
—help us to make up for our sins against your wisdom and goodness.

Cleanse and renew your Church, Lord,
—may it grow in strength as a witness to you.

Touch the hearts of those who have abandoned you through sin and scandal,
—call them back to you and keep them faithful in your love.

May we show forth in our lives the sufferings of your Son,
—you raised us up to life when you raised him from the dead.

Have mercy on us, Lord, as we praise and thank you,
—with your pardon give us also your peace.

Lord, our sins are many, but we trust in your mercy,
—call us, and we shall turn to you.

Receive us as we come before you with humble and contrite hearts,
—those who trust in you shall never trust in vain.

We have turned away from you and fallen into sin,
—we have followed evil ways and rejected your commandments.

Turn to us, Lord, and show us your mercy; blot out our sins,
—cast them into the depths of the sea.

Restore us, Lord, to your favor, and give us joy in your presence,
—may our glory be to serve you with all our hearts.

Or:

If the prayer is addressed to Christ: [205]

1

—By your death you reconciled us with the Father and brought us salvation.   *(Romans 5:10)*

R.   Lord, have mercy.   *Or:* Christ, hear us.

Or another suitable response may be used.

—You died and rose again, and sit at the right hand of the Father, to make intercession for us.   R.
(Romans 8:34)

—You came from God as our wisdom and justice, our sanctification and redemption. R. *(1 Corinthians 1:30)*

—You washed mankind in the Spirit of our God; you made us holy and righteous.   R.   *(1 Corinthians 6:11)*

—You warned us that if we sin against each other we sin against you.   R. *(1 Corinthians 8:12)*

—Though you were rich you became poor for our sake, so that by your poverty we might become rich. R.   *(2 Corinthians 8:9)*

—You gave yourself up for our sins to save us from this evil world. R.   *(Galatians 1:4)*

—You rose from the dead to save us from the anger that was to come. R.   *(1 Thessalonians 1:10)*

—You came into the world to save sinners. R.
(1 Timothy 1:15)

—You gave yourself up to bring redemption to all. R.   *(1 Timothy 2:6)*

—You destroyed death and gave light to life. R.
(2 Timothy 1:10)

—You will come to judge the living and the dead. R.
(2 Timothy 4:1)

—You gave yourself up for us to redeem us from all sin and to prepare for yourself a holy people, marked as your own, devoted to good works. R. *(Titus 2:14)*

—You showed us your mercy, and as a faithful high priest in the things of God you made atonement for the sins of the people. R. *(Hebrews 2:17)*

—You became the source of salvation for all who obey you. R. *(Hebrews 5:9)*

—Through the Holy Spirit you offered yourself to God as a spotless victim, cleansing our consciences from lifeless works. R. *(Hebrews 9:15)*

—You were offered in sacrifice to undo the sins of the many. R. *(Hebrews 9:28)*

—Once and for all you died for our sins, the innocent one for the guilty. R. *(1 Peter 3:18)*

—You are the atonement for our sins and for the sins of the world. R. *(1 John 2:2)*

—You died that those who believe in you may not perish but have eternal life. R. *(John 3:16, 35)*

—You came into the world to seek and save what was lost. R. *(Matthew 18:11)*

—You were sent by the Father, not to judge the world but to save it. R. *(John 3:17)*

—You have power on earth to forgive sins. R.
(Mark 2:10)

—You invite all who labor and are burdened to come to you to be refreshed. R. *(Matthew 11:28)*

—You gave your apostles the keys of the kingdom of heaven, the power to bind and to loose. R.
(Matthew 16:19; 18:18)

—You told us that the whole law depends on love of God and of our neighbor. R. *(Matthew 22:38-40)*

—Jesus, life of all mankind, you came into the world to give us life, life in its fullness. R. *(John 10:10)*

—Jesus, Good Shepherd, you gave your life for your sheep. R. *(John 10:11)*

—Jesus, eternal truth, you give us true freedom.   R.
(John 14:6; 8:32, 36)

—Jesus, you are the way to the Father.   R.   *(John 14:6)*

—Jesus, you are the resurrection and life; those who believe in you, even if they are dead, will live.   R.
(John 11:25)

—Jesus, true vine, the Father prunes your branches to make them bear even greater fruit.   R.   *(John 15:1-2)*

2

The following intercessions may be used with a variable response or with an invariable response as in the Liturgy of the Hours.

Healer of body and soul, bind up the wounds of our hearts,
—that our lives may grow strong through grace.

Help us to strip ourselves of sin,
—and put on the new life of grace.

Redeemer of the world, give us the spirit of penance and a deeper devotion to your passion,
—so that we may have a fuller share in your risen glory.

May your Mother, the refuge of sinners, intercede for us,
—and ask you in your goodness to pardon our sins.

You forgave the woman who repented,
—show us also your mercy.

211

You brought back the lost sheep on your shoulders,
—pity us and lead us home.

You promised paradise to the good thief,
—take us with you into your Kingdom.

You died for us and rose again,
—make us share in your death and resurrection.

55.   *Individual Confession and Absolution*

*Then the penitents go to the priests designated
for individual confession, and confess their sins. Each
one receives and accepts a fitting act of satisfaction and is absolved. After hearing the confession
and offering suitable counsel, the priest extends
his hands over the penitent's head (or at least extends
his right hand), and gives him absolution. Everything
else which is customary in individual confession is
omitted.*

God, the Father of mercies,
through the death and resurrection of his Son
has reconciled the world to himself
and sent the Holy Spirit among us
for the forgiveness of sins;
through the ministry of the Church
may God give you pardon and peace,
and I absolve you from your sins
in the name of the Father, and of the Son,+
and of the Holy Spirit.

    The penitent answers:

R.   Amen.

56.   *Proclamation of Praise for God's mercy*

When the individual confessions have been completed, the other priests stand with the one who is presiding over the celebration. The latter invites all present to offer thanks and encourages them to do good works which will proclaim the grace of repentance in the life of the entire community and each of its members. It is fitting for all to sing a psalm or hymn or to say a litany in acknowledgment of God's power and mercy, for example, the canticle of Mary (Luke 1:46-55), or Psalm 136:1-9, 13-14, 16, 25-26.

Or:

PROCLAMATION OF PRAISE   [206]

Psalm 32:1-7, 10-11
R.   Rejoice in the Lord and sing for joy, friends of God.

Psalm 98:1-9
R.   The Lord has remembered his mercy.

Psalm 100:2-5
R.   The Lord is loving and kind: his mercy is for ever.

Psalm 119:1, 10-13, 15-16, 18, 33, 105, 169, 170, 174-175.
R.   Blessed are you, Lord; teach me your decrees.

Psalm 103:1-4, 8-18
R.   The mercy of the Lord is from everlasting to everlasting on those who revere him.

Psalm 145:1-21
R.   Day after day I will bless you, Lord: I will praise your name for ever.

Psalm 146:2-10
R.   I will sing to my God all the days of my life.

Isaiah 12:1b-6
R.   Praise the Lord and call upon his name.

Isaiah 61:10-11
R.   My spirit rejoices in my God.

Jeremiah 31:10-14
R.   The Lord has redeemed his people.

Daniel 3:52-57
R.   Bless the Lord, all the works of his hand: praise
      and glorify him for ever.

Luke 1:46-55
R.   The Lord has remembered his mercy.

Ephesians 1:3-10
R.   Blessed be God who chose us in Christ.

Revelation 15:3-4
R.   Great and wonderful are all your works, Lord.

57.   *Concluding Prayer of Thanksgiving*

      *After the song of praise or the litany, the priest
      concludes the common prayer:*

Almighty and merciful God,
how wonderfully you created man
and still more wonderfully remade him.
You do not abandon the sinner
but seek him out with a father's love.
You sent your Son into the world
to destroy sin and death
by his passion,

and to restore life and joy
by his resurrection.
You sent the Holy Spirit into our hearts
to make us your children
and heirs of your kingdom.
You constantly renew our spirit
in the sacraments of your redeeming love,
freeing us from slavery to sin
and transforming us ever more closely
into the likeness of your beloved Son.
We thank you for the wonders of your mercy,
and with heart and hand and voice
we join with the whole Church
in a new song of praise:
Glory to you
through Christ
in the Holy Spirit,
now and for ever.

R.   Amen.

Or:

All-holy Father,
you have shown us your mercy
and made us a new creation
in the likeness of your Son.
Make us living signs of your love
for the whole world to see.

We ask this through Christ our Lord.

R.   Amen.

Or:

Father, all-powerful and ever-living God,   [207]
we do well aways and everywhere to give you thanks.

215

When you punish us, you show your justice;
when you pardon us, you show your kindness;
yet always your mercy enfolds us.

When you chastise us, you do not wish to condemn us;
when you spare us, you give us time to make amends
      for our sins
through Christ our Lord.

R.   Amen.

Or:

Lord God,   [208]
creator and ruler of your kingdom of light,
in your great love for this world
you gave up your only Son
for our salvation.
His cross has redeemed us,
his death has given us life,
his resurrection has raised us to glory.
Through him we ask you
to be always present among your family.
Teach us to be reverent in the presence of your glory;
fill our hearts with faith,
our days with good works,
our lives with your love;
may your truth be on our lips
and your wisdom in all our actions,
that we may receive the reward of everlasting life.

We ask this through Christ our Lord.

R.   Amen.

Or:

Lord Jesus Christ,   [209]
your loving forgiveness knows no limits.
You took our human nature
to give us an example of humility
and to make us faithful in every trial.
May we never lose the gifts you have given us,
but if we fall into sin,
lift us up by your gift of repentance,
for you live and reign for ever and ever.

R.   Amen.

Or:

Father,   [210]
in your love you have brought us
from evil to good and from misery to happiness.
Through your blessings
give the courage of perseverance
to those you have called and justified by faith.

Grant this through Christ our Lord.

R.   Amen.

Or:

God and Father of us all,   [211]
you have forgiven our sins
and sent us your peace.
Help us to forgive each other
and to work together to establish peace in the world.

We ask this through Christ our Lord.

R.   Amen.

Concluding Rite

58. *Then the priest blesses all present:*

May the Lord guide your hearts in the way of his love
and fill you with Christ-like patience.

R.   Amen.

May he give you strength
to walk in newness of life
and to please him in all things.

R.   Amen.

May almighty God bless you,
the Father, and the Son, + and the Holy Spirit.

R.   Amen.

Or:

And may the blessing of almighty God,   [212]
the Father, and the Son, + and the Holy Spirit,
come upon you and remain with you for ever.

R.   Amen.

Or:

May the Father bless us,   [213]
for we are his children, born to eternal life.

R.   Amen.

May the Son show us his saving power,
for he died and rose for us.

R.   Amen.

May the Spirit give us his gift of holiness
and lead us by the right path,
for he dwells in our hearts.

R.   Amen.

Or:

May the Father bless us,   [214]
for he has adopted us to be his children.

R.   Amen.

May the Son come to help us,
for he has received us as brothers and sisters.

R.   Amen.

May the Spirit be with us,
for he has made us his dwelling place.

R.   Amen.

59.   *The deacon or other minister or the priest
        himself dismisses the assembly:*

The Lord has freed you from your sins. Go in peace.

        All answer:

Thanks be to God.

        Any other appropriate form may be used.

Chapter III

RITE FOR RECONCILIATION OF SEVERAL PENITENTS WITH GENERAL CONFESSION AND ABSOLUTION

60.   For the reconciliation of several penitents with general confession and absolution, in the cases provided for in the law, everything is done as described above for the reconciliation of several penitents with individual absolution, but with the following changes only.

Instruction

After the homily or as part of the homily, the priest explains to the faithful who wish to receive general absolution that they should be properly disposed. Each one should repent of his sins and resolve to turn away from these sins, to make up for any scandal and harm he may have caused, and to confess individually at the proper time each of the serious sins, which cannot now be confessed. Some form of satisfaction should be proposed to all, and each individual may add something if he desires.

General Confession

61.   Then the deacon or other minister or the priest himself invites the penitents who wish to receive absolution to indicate this by some kind of sign. He may say:

Will those of you who wish to receive sacramental absolution please kneel and acknowledge that you are sinners.

Or:

Will those of you who wish to receive sacramental absolution please bow your heads and acknowledge that you are sinners.

Or he may suggest a sign as laid down by the episcopal conference.

The penitents say a general formula for confession (for example, I confess to almighty God). *A litany or appropriate song may follow, as described above for the reconciliation of several penitents with individual confession and absolution (no. 54). The Lord's Prayer is always added at the end.*

General Absolution

62. *The priest then gives absolution, holding his hands extended over the penitents and saying:*

God the Father does not wish the sinner to die
but to turn back to him and live.
He loved us first and sent his Son into the world to be
    its Savior.
May he show you his merciful love and give you peace.

R.   Amen.

Our Lord Jesus Christ was given up to death for our
    sins,
and rose again for our justification.
He sent the Holy Spirit on his apostles
and gave them power to forgive sins.

Through the ministry entrusted to me
may he deliver you from evil
and fill you with his Holy Spirit.

R.   Amen.

The Spirit, the Comforter, was given to us for the for-
     giveness of sins.
In him we approach the Father.
May he cleanse your hearts and clothe you in his glory,
so that you may proclaim the mighty acts of God,
who has called you out of darkness into the splendor
     of his light.

R.   Amen.

And I absolve you from your sins
in the name of the Father, and of the Son, +
and of the Holy Spirit.

R.   Amen.

Or:

God, the Father of mercies,
through the death and resurrection of his Son
has reconciled the world to himself
and sent the Holy Spirit among us
for the forgiveness of sins;
through the ministry of the Church
may God give you pardon and peace,
and I absolve you from your sins
in the name of the Father, and of the Son, +
and of the Holy Spirit.

R.   Amen.

63.   *Proclamation of Praise and Conclusion*

The priest invites all to thank God and to ac-
knowledge his mercy. After a suitable song or hymn,
he blesses the people and dismisses them, as described
above, nos. 58-59, but without the concluding prayer
(no. 57).

SHORT RITE

64.   *In case of necessity, the rite for reconciling*
several penitents with general confession and absolu-
tion may be shortened. If possible, there is a brief
reading from scripture. After giving the usual instruc-
tion (no. 60) and indicating the act of penance, the
priest invites the penitents to make a general confes-
sion (for example, I confess to almighty God), *and gives*
the absolution with the form which is indicated in No.
62.

65.   *In imminent danger of death, it is enough for the*
priest to use the form of absolution itself. In this case
it may be shortened to the following:

> I absolve you from your sins
> in the name of the Father, and of the Son, +
> and of the Holy Spirit.
>
> R.   Amen.

66.   *A person who receives general absolution from*
grave sins is bound to confess each grave sin at his next
individual confession.

Chapter IV

VARIOUS TEXTS USED IN THE CELEBRATION OF RECONCILIATION

(All the various texts used in the celebration of reconciliation, except the list of biblical readings, appear in their proper places under the various rites and are not repeated here. The list of biblical readings follows with page references to where each can be found in this book.)

BIBLICAL READINGS

The following readings are proposed as a help for pastors and others involved in the selection of readings. For diversity, and according to the nature of the group, other readings may be selected.

READINGS FROM THE OLD TESTAMENT

101. *Genesis 3:1-19* She took the fruit of the tree and ate it. (pp. 35-37)
102. *Genesis 4:1-15* Cain set on his brother and killed him. (pp. 37-38)
103. *Genesis 18:17-33* The Lord said: I will not destroy the city for the sake of ten good men. (pp. 234-235)
104. *Exodus 17:1-7* They tempted the Lord saying: Is the Lord here or not? (p. 235)
105. *Exodus 20:1-21* I am the Lord your God . . . you will not have other gods. (pp. 38-39)
106. *Deuteronomy 6:3-9* Love the Lord your God with your whole heart. (p. 235)

107. *Deuteronomy 9:7-19* Your people quickly turned away from the wrong you had showed them. (pp. 235-236)

108. *Deuteronomy 30:15-20* I set before you life and prosperity, death and evil. (pp. 236-237)

109. *2 Samuel 12:1-9, 13* David said to Nathan: I have sinned against the Lord God. Nathan said to David: The Lord has forgiven your sin; you will not die. (p. 237)

110. *Nehemiah 9:1-20* The sons of Israel assembled for a fast and confessed their sins. (pp. 237-239)

111. *Wisdom 1:1-16* Love justice, for wisdom will not enter an evil soul nor live in a body subjected to sin. (pp. 239-240)

112. *Wisdom 5:1-16* The hope of the wicked is like down flying on the wind. The just, however, live for ever. (pp. 240-241)

113. *Sirach 28:1-7* Forgive your neighbor when he hurts you, and then your sins will be forgiven when you pray. (pp. 241-242)

114. *Isaiah 1:2-6, 15-18* I have nourished and educated sons; however they have rebelled against me. (p. 242)

115. *Isaiah 5:1-7* The vineyard became my delight. He looked for grapes, but it yielded wild grapes. (pp. 242-243)

116. *Isaiah 43:22-28* On account of me your iniquities are blotted out. (p. 243)

117. *Isaiah 53:1-12* The Lord laid upon him our guilt. (pp. 22-23)

118. *Isaiah 55:1-11* Let the wicked man forsake his way and return to the Lord, and he will have mercy on him because he is generous in forgiving. (pp. 26-28)

119. *Isaiah 58:1-11* When you give your bread to the hungry and fulfill the troubled soul, your light will rise like dawn from the darkness, and your

darkness will be like midday. (pp. 99-100)

120. *Isaiah 59:1-4, 9-15* Your iniquities divide you and your God. (pp. 243-244)

121. *Jeremiah 2:1-13* My people have done two evils: they have abandoned me, the fountain of living water, and have dug for themselves broken cisterns which hold no water. (pp. 244-245)

122. *Jeremiah 7:21-26* Listen to my voice, and I will be your God, and you will be my people. (p. 245)

123. *Ezekiel 11:14-21* I will take the heart of stone from their bodies, and I will give them a heart of flesh, so that they may walk according to my laws. (p. 246)

124. *Ezekiel 18:20-32* If a wicked man turns away from his sins, he shall live and not die. (pp. 23-24)

125. *Ezekiel 36:23-28* I shall sprinkle upon you clean water, put my spirit within you, and make you walk according to my commands. (p. 246)

126. *Hosea 2:16-25* I will make a covenant for them on that day. (pp. 246-247)

127. *Hosea 11:1-11* I took them in my arms, and they did not know that I cured them. (pp. 247-248)

128. *Hosea 14:2-10* Israel, return to the Lord your God. (p. 248)

129. *Joel 2:12-19* Return to me with your whole heart. (pp. 28-29)

130. *Micah 6:1-4, 6-8* Do right and love mercy, and walk humbly with your God. (p. 249)

131. *Ezekiel 36:23-28* The Lord will turn back and have mercy on us; he will cast all our sins into the depths of the sea. (p. 246)

132. *Zechariah 1:1-6* Return to me, and I shall return to you. (p. 249)

RESPONSORIAL PSALM

133. *Psalm 12* (Ps 13, p. 250)
R. *(6a):* All my hope, O Lord, is in your loving kindness.

134. *Psalm 24* (Ps 25, pp. 250-251)
R. *(16a):* Turn to me, Lord, and have mercy.

135. *Psalm 30:1-6* (Ps 31, p. 251)
R. *(6b):* You have redeemed us, Lord, God of truth.

136. *Psalm 31* (Ps 32, pp. 73-74)
R. *(5c):* Lord, forgive the wrong I have done.

137. *Psalm 35* (Ps 36, pp. 251-252)
R. *(8):* How precious is your unfailing love, Lord.

138. *Psalm 49:7-8, 14-23* (Ps 50, pp. 252-253)
R. *(23b):* To the upright I will show the saving power of God.

139. *Psalm 50* (Ps 51, pp. 74-76)
R. *(14a):* Give back to me the joy of your salvation.

140. *Psalm 72* (Ps 73, pp. 253-254)
R. *(28a):* It is good for me to be with the Lord.

141. *Psalm 89* (Ps 90, pp. 254-255)
R. *(14):* Fill us with your love, O Lord, and we will sing for joy!

142. *Psalm 94* (Ps 95, pp. 255-256)
R. *(8a):* If today you hear his voice, harden not your hearts.

143. *Psalm 118:1, 10-13, 15-16* (Ps 119, p. 256)
R. *(1):* Happy are they who follow the law of the Lord!

144. *Psalm 122* (Ps 123, pp. 256-257)
R. *(2c):* Our eyes are fixed on the Lord.

145. *Psalm 129* (Ps 130, pp. 13-14)
R. *(7bc):* With the Lord there is mercy, and fullness of redemption.

146. *Psalm 138:1-18, 23-24* (Ps 139, pp. 257-258)

R. *(23a):* You have searched me, and you
know me, Lord.
147. *Psalm 142:1-11* (Ps 143, pp. 76-77)
R. *(10):* Teach me to do your will, my God.

READINGS FROM THE NEW TESTAMENT

148. *Romans 3:22-26* All men are justified by the gift
of God through redemption in Christ Jesus.
(p. 258)
149. *Romans 5:6-11* We give glory in God through
our Lord Jesus Christ, through whom we have
received reconciliation. (pp. 21-22)
150. *Romans 6:2b-13* Consider yourselves dead to
sin but alive to God. (pp. 84-85)
151. *Romans 6:16-23* The wages of sin is death; the
gift of God is eternal life in Christ Jesus our
Lord. (p. 85)
152. *Romans 7:14-25* Unhappy man am I! Who will
free me? Thanks to God through Jesus Christ
our Lord. (p. 86)
153. *Romans 12:1-2, 9-19* Be transformed by the renewal of your mind. (pp. 87-88)
154. *Romans 13:8-14* Let us cast away the works of
darkness and put on the weapons of light.
(p. 259)
155. *2 Corinthians 5:17-21* God reconciled the world
to himself through Christ. (p. 259)
156. *Galatians 5:16-24* You cannot belong to Christ
unless you crucify the flesh with its passions
and concupiscence. (pp. 41-42)
157. *Ephesians 2:1-10* When we were dead to sin,
God, on account of his great love for us,
brought us to life in Christ. (pp. 88-89)
158. *Ephesians 4:1-3, 17-32* Renew yourself and put
on the new man. (pp. 89-90)
159. *Ephesians 5:1-14* You were once in darkness;

now you are light in the Lord, so walk as children of light. (pp. 42-43)

160. *Ephesians 6:10-18* Put God's armor on so that you will be able to stand firm against evil. (p. 46)

161. *Colossians 3:1-10, 12-17* If you were raised to life with Christ, aspire to the realm above. Put to death what remains in this earthly life. (pp. 91-92)

162. *Hebrews 12:1-5* You have not resisted to the point of shedding your blood in your struggle against sin. (pp. 259-260)

163. *James 1:22-27* Be doers of the word and not merely listeners. (p. 93)

164. *James 2:14-26* What use is it if someone says that he believes and does not manifest it in works? (pp. 93-94)

165. *James 3:1-12* If someone does not offend in word, he is a perfect man. (pp. 49-50)

166. *1 Peter 1:13-23* You have been redeemed not by perishable goods, gold or silver, but by the precious blood of Jesus Christ. (p. 260)

167. *2 Peter 1:3-11* Be careful so that you may make firm your calling and election. (pp. 260-261)

168. *1 John 1:5-10; 2:1-2* If we confess our sins, he is faithful and just and will forgive our sins and cleanse us from all injustice. (p. 261)

169. *John 2:3-11* Whoever hates his brother remains in darkness. (p. 262)

170. *1 John 3:1-24* We know that we have crossed over from death to life because we love our brothers. (pp. 94-96)

171. *1 John 4:16-21* God is love, and he who lives in love, lives in God, and God in him. (pp. 96-98)

229

Appendix I

ABSOLUTION FROM CENSURES

1.   *The form of absolution is not to be changed in respect to sins which are now reserved either in themselves or by reason of a censure. It is enough that the confessor intend to absolve the properly disposed penitent from these reserved sins. Until other provision is made and as may be necessary, the present regulations which make recourse to the competent authority obligatory are to be observed. Before absolving from sins, however, the confessor may absolve from the censure, using the formula which is given below for absolution from censure outside the sacrament of penance.*

2.   *When a priest, in accordance with the law, absolves a penitent from a censure outside the sacrament of penance, he uses the following formula:*

By the power granted to me,
I absolve you
from the bond of excommunication
   (or *suspension* or *interdict*).
In the name of the Father, and of the Son, +
and of the Holy Spirit.

The penitent answers:

Amen.

DISPENSATION FROM IRREGULARITY

3.   *When, in accordance with the law, a priest dispenses a penitent from an irregularity, either during confession, after absolution has been given, or outside the sacrament of penance, he says:*

By the power granted to me
I dispense you from the irregularity
which you have incurred.
In the name of the Father, and of the Son, +
and of the Holy Spirit.

The penitent answers:

Amen.

TEXTS OF BIBLICAL READINGS

101.   Gn 3:1-19 (pp. 35-37)
102.   Gn 4:1-15 (pp. 37-38)
103.   Gn 18:17-33

The Lord reflected. "Shall I hide from Abraham what I am about to do, now that he is to become a great and populous nation, and all the nations of the earth are to find blessing in him? Indeed, I have singled him out that he may direct his sons and his posterity to keep the way of the Lord by doing what is right and just, so that the Lord may carry into effect for Abraham the promises he made about him." Then the Lord said: "The outcry against Sodom and Gomorrah is so great, and their sin so grave, that I must go down and see whether or not their actions fully correspond to the cry against them that comes to me. I mean to find out."

While the two men walked on farther toward Sodom, the Lord remained standing before Abraham. Then Abraham drew nearer to him and said: "Will you sweep away the innocent with the guilty. Suppose there were fifty innocent people in the city; would you wipe out the place, rather than spare it for the sake of the fifty innocent people within it? Far be it from you to do such a thing, to make the innocent die with the guilty, so that the innocent and the guilty would be treated alike! Should not the judge of all the world act with justice?" The Lord replied, "If I find fifty innocent people in the city of Sodom, I will spare the whole place for their sake. Abraham spoke up again: "See how I am presuming to speak to my Lord, though I am but dust and ashes! What if there are five less than fifty innocent people? Will you destroy the whole city because of those five?" "I will not destroy it," he answered, "if I find forty-five there." But Abraham persisted, saying, "What if only forty are found there?" He replied, "I will forbear doing it for the sake of the forty." Then he said, "Let not my Lord grow impatient if I go on. What if only thirty are found there?" He replied, "I will forbear doing it if I can find but thirty there." Still he went on, "Since I have thus dared to speak to my Lord, what if there are no

234

more than twenty?" "I will not destroy it," he answered, "for the sake of the twenty." But he still persisted: "Please, let not my Lord grow angry if I speak up this last time. What if there are at least ten there?" "For the sake of those ten," he replied, "I will not destroy it."

The Lord departed as soon as he had finished speaking with Abraham, and Abraham returned home.

104. Ex 17:1-7

From the desert of Sin the whole Israelite community journeyed by stages, as the Lord directed, and encamped at Rephidim.

Here there was no water for the people to drink. They quarreled, therefore, with Moses and said, "Give us water to drink." Moses replied, "Why do you quarrel with me? Why do you put the Lord to a test?" Here, then, in their thirst for water, the people grumbled against Moses, saying, "Why did you ever make us leave Egypt? Was it just to have us die here of thirst with our children and our livestock?" So Moses cried out to the Lord, "What shall I do with this people? A little more and they will stone me!" The Lord answered Moses, "Go over there in front of the people, along with some of the elders of Israel, holding in your hand, as you go, the staff with which you struck the river. I will be standing there in front of you on the rock in Horeb. Strike the rock, and the water will flow from it for the people to drink." This Moses did, in the presence of the elders of Israel. The place was called Massah and Meribah, because the Israelites quarreled there and tested the Lord, saying, "Is the Lord in our midst or not?"

105. Ex 20:1-21 (pp. 38-39)
106. Dt 6:4-9

"Hear, O Israel! The Lord is our God, the Lord alone! Therefore, you shall love the Lord, your God, with all your heart, and with all your soul and with all your strength. Take to heart these words which I enjoin on you today. Drill them into your children. Speak of them at home and abroad, whether you are busy or at rest. Bind them at your wrist as a sign and let them be as a pendant on your forehead. Write them on the doorposts of your houses and on your gates."

107. Dt 9:7-19

"Bear in mind and do not forget how you angered the Lord, your God, in the desert. From the day you left the land of Egypt until you arrived in this place, you have been rebellious toward the Lord. At Horeb you so provoked the Lord that he was angry enough to destroy you, when I had gone up the mountain to receive the stone tablets of the covenant which the Lord made with you. Meanwhile I stayed on the mountain forty day and forty nights without eating or drinking, till the Lord gave me the two tablets of stone inscribed, by God's own finger, with a copy of all the words that the Lord spoke to you on the mountain from the midst of the fire on the day of the assembly. Then, at the end of the forty days and forty nights, when the Lord had given me the two stone tablets of the covenant, he said to me, 'Go down from here now, quickly, for your people whom you have brought out of Egypt have become depraved; they have already turned aside from the way I pointed out to them and have made for themselves a molten idol. I have seen now how stiff-necked this people is,' the Lord said to me. 'Let me be, that I may destroy them and blot out their name from under the heavens. I will then make of you a nation mightier and greater than they.'

"When I had come down again from the blazing, fiery mountain, with the two tablets of the covenant in both my hands, I saw how you had sinned against the Lord, your God: you had already turned aside from the way which the Lord had pointed out to you by making for yourselves a molten calf! Raising the two tablets with both hands I threw them from me and broke them before your eyes. Then, as before, I lay prostrate before the Lord for forty days and forty nights without eating or drinking, because of all the sin you had committed in the sight of the Lord and the evil you had done to provoke him. For I dreaded the fierce anger of the Lord against you: his wrath would destroy you. Yet once again the Lord listened to me."

108.   Dt 30:15-20

"Here, then, I have today set before you life and prosperity, death and doom. If you obey the commandments of the Lord, your God, which I enjoin on you today, loving him, and walking in his ways, and keeping his commandments, statutes and decrees, you will live and grow numerous, and the Lord, your God, will bless you in the land you are entering to occupy. If, however, you turn away your hearts and will not listen, but are led astray and adore and serve other gods, I tell you now that you will certainly perish; you will not have a long life on the land which

you are crossing the Jordan to enter and occupy. I call heaven
and earth today to witness against you: I have set before you
life and death, the blessing and the curse. Choose life, then, that
you and your descendants may live, by loving the Lord, your
God, heeding his voice, and holding fast to him. For that will
mean life for you, a long life for you to live on the land which
the Lord swore he would give to your fathers Abraham, Isaac
and Jacob."

109. 2 Sm 12:1-9, 13

The Lord sent Nathan to David, and when he came to him, he
said: "Judge this case for me! In a certain town there were two
men, one rich, the other poor. The rich man had flocks and
herds in great numbers. But the poor man had nothing at all
except one little ewe lamb that he had bought. He nourished
her, and she grew up with him and his children. She shared the
little food he had and drank from his cup and slept in his bosom.
She was like a daughter to him. Now, the rich man received a
visitor, but he would not take from his own flocks and herds to
prepare a meal for the wayfarer who had come to him. Instead
he took the poor man's ewe lamb and made a meal of it for his
visitor." David grew very angry with that man and said to
Nathan: "As the Lord lives, the man who has done this merits
death! He shall restore the ewe lamb fourfold because he has
done this and has had no pity."

Then Nathan said to David: "You are the man! Thus says the
Lord God of Israel: 'I anointed you king of Israel. I rescued you
from the hand of Saul. I gave you your lord's house and your
lord's wives for your own. I gave you the house of Israel and of
Judah. And if this were not enough, I could count up for you
still more. Why have you spurned the Lord and done evil in
his sight? You have cut down Uriah the Hittite with the sword;
you took his wife as your own, and him you killed with the
sword of the Ammonites.' " . . . Then David said to Nathan, "I . .
have sinned against the Lord." Nathan answered David: "The Lord
on his part has forgiven your sin: you shall not die."

110. Neh 9:1-20

On the twenty-fourth day of this month, the Israelites
gathered together fasting and in sackcloth, their heads covered
with dust. Those of Israelite descent separated themselves from

all who were of foreign extraction, then stood forward and confessed their sins and the guilty deeds of their fathers. When they had taken their places, they read from the book of the law of the Lord their God, for a fourth part of the day, and during another fourth part they made their confession and prostrated themselves before the Lord their God. Standing on the platform of the Levites were Jeshua, Binnui, Kadmiel, Shebaniah, Bunni, Sherebiah, Bani, and Chenani, who cried out to the Lord their God, with a loud voice. The Levites Jeshua, Kadmiel, Bani, Hashabneiah, Sherebiah, Hodiah, Shebaniah, and Pethahiah said,

"Arise, bless the Lord, your God,
  from eternity to eternity!"

The Israelites answered with the blessing,

"Blessed is your glorious name,
  and exalted above all blessing and praise."

Then Ezra said: "It is you, O Lord, you are the only one; you made the heavens, the highest heavens and all their host, the earth and all that is upon it, the seas and all that is in them. To all of them you give life, and the heavenly hosts bow down before you.
  "You, O Lord, are the God who chose Abram, who brought him out of Ur of the Chaldees, and named him Abraham. When you had found his heart faithful in your sight, you made the covenant with him to give to him and his posterity the land of the Canaanites, Hittites, Amorites, Perizzites, Jebusites, and Girgashites. These promises of yours you fulfilled, for you are just.

"You saw the affliction of our fathers in Egypt,
  you heard their cry by the Red Sea;
You worked signs and wonders against Pharaoh,
  against all his servants and the people of his land,
Because you knew of their insolence toward them;
  thus you made for yourself a name even to this day.
The sea you divided before them,
  on dry ground they passed through the midst of the sea;
Their pursuers you hurled into the depths,
  like a stone into the mighty waters.
With a column of cloud you led them by day,
  and by night with a column of fire,
To light the way of their journey,

the way in which they must travel.
On Mount Sinai you came down,
  you spoke with them from heaven;
You gave them just ordinances, firm laws,
  good statutes, and commandments;
Your holy Sabbath you made known to them,
  commandments, statutes, and law you prescribed for them,
  by the hand of Moses your servant.
Food from heaven you gave them in their hunger,
  water from a rock you sent them in their thirst.
You bade them enter and occupy the land
  which you had sworn with upraised hand to give them.

"But they, our fathers, proved to be insolent; they held their necks stiff and would not obey your commandments. They refused to obey and no longer remembered the miracles you had worked for them. They stiffened their necks and turned their heads to return to their slavery in Egypt. But you are a God of pardons, gracious and compassionate, slow to anger and rich in mercy; you did not forsake them. Though they made for themselves a molten calf, and proclaimed, 'Here is your God who brought you up out of Egypt,' and were guilty of great effronteries, yet in your great mercy you did not forsake them in the desert. The column of cloud did not cease to lead them by day on their journey, nor did the column of fire by night cease to light for them the way by which they were to travel.

"Your good spirit you bestowed on them, to give them understanding; your manna you did not withhold from their mouths, and you gave them water in their thirst."

111. Wis 1:1-16
Love justice, you who judge the earth;
  think of the Lord in goodness,
  and seek him in integrity of heart;
Because he is found by those who test him not,
  and he manifests himself to those who do not disbelieve him.
For perverse counsels separate a man from God,
  and his power, put to the proof, rebukes the foolhardy;
Because into a soul that plots evil wisdom enters not,
  nor dwells she in a body under debt of sin.
For the holy spirit of discipline flees deceit
  and withdraws from senseless counsels;
  and when injustice occurs it is rebuked.
For wisdom is a kindly spirit,
  yet she acquits not the blasphemer of his guilty lips;

Because God is the witness of his inmost self
  and the sure observer of his heart and the listener to his tongue.
For the spirit of the Lord fills the world,
  is all-embracing, and knows what man says.
Therefore no one who utters wicked things can go unnoticed,
  nor will chastising condemnation pass him by.
For the devices of the wicked man shall be scrutinized,
  and the sound of his words shall reach the Lord,
  for the chastisement of his transgressions;
Because a jealous ear hearkens to everything,
  and discordant grumblings are no secret.
Therefore guard against profitless grumbling,
  and from calumny withhold your tongues;
For a stealthy utterance does not go unpunished,
  and a lying mouth slays the soul.
Court not death by your erring way of life,
  nor draw to yourselves destruction by the works of your hands.
Because God did not make death,
  nor does he rejoice in the destruction of the living.
For he fashioned all things that they might have being;
  and the creatures of the world are wholesome,
And there is not a destructive drug among them
  nor any domain of the nether world on earth,
For justice is undying.
It was the wicked who with hands and words invited death,
  considered it a friend, and pined for it,
  and made a covenant with it,
Because they deserve to be in its possession.

112. Wis 5:1-16
Then shall the just one with great assurance confront
  his oppressors who set at nought his labors.
Seeing this, they shall be shaken with dreadful fear,
  and amazed at the unlooked-for salvation.
They shall say among themselves, rueful
  and groaning through anguish of spirit:
"This is he whom once we held as a laughingstock
  and as a type for mockery, fools that we were!
His life we accounted madness, and his death dishonored.
See how he is accounted among the sons of God;
  how his lot is with the saints!
We, then, have strayed from the way of truth,
  and the light of justice did not shine for us,
  and the sun did not rise for us.

240

We had our fill of the ways of mischief and of ruin;
　　we journeyed through impassable deserts,
　　but the way of the Lord we knew not.
What did our pride avail us?
　　What have wealth and its boastfulness afforded us?
All of them passed like a shadow and like a fleeting rumor;
Like a ship traversing the heaving water,
　　of which, when it has passed, no trace can be found,
　　no path of its keel in the waves.
Or like a bird flying through the air;
　　no evidence of its course is to be found—
But the fluid air, lashed by the beat of pinions,
　　and cleft by the rushing force
Of speeding wings, is traversed: and afterward no mark of
　　passage can be found in it.
Or as, when an arrow has been shot at a mark,
　　the parted air straightway flows together again
　　so that none discerns the way it went through—
Even so we, once born, abruptly came to nought
　　and held no sign of virtue to display,
　　but were consumed in our wickedness."
Yes, the hope of the wicked is like thistledown borne on the wind,
　　and like fine, tempest-driven foam;
Like smoke scattered by the wind,
　　and like the passing memory of the nomad camping for a
　　　　single day.
But the just live forever, and in the Lord is their recompense,
　　and the thought of them is with the Most High.
Therefore shall they receive the splendid crown,
　　the beauteous diadem, from the hand of the Lord—
For he shall shelter them with his right hand,
　　and protect them with his arm.

113.　Sir 28:1-7
The vengeful will suffer the Lord's vengeance,
　　for he remembers their sins in detail.
Forgive your neighbor's injustice;
　　then when you pray, your own sins will be forgiven.
Should a man nourish anger against his fellows
　　and expect healing from the Lord?
Should a man refuse mercy to his fellows,
　　yet seek pardon for his own sins?
If he who is but flesh cherishes wrath,
　　who will forgive his sins?

Remember your last days, set enmity aside;
  remember death and decay, and cease from sin!
Think of the commandments, hate not your neighbor;
  of the Most High's covenant, and overlook faults.

114.   Is 1:2-6, 15-18
Hear, O heavens, and listen, O earth,
  for the Lord speaks:
Sons have I raised and reared, but they have disowned me!
An ox knows its owner, and an ass, its master's manger;
But Israel does not know, my people has not understood.
Ah! sinful nation, people laden with wickedness,
  evil race, corrupt children!
They have forsaken the Lord, spurned the Holy One of
  Israel, apostatized.
Where would you yet be struck, you that rebel again and again?
The whole head is sick, the whole heart faint.
From the sole of the foot to the head
  there is no sound spot:
Wound and welt and gaping gash,
  not drained, or bandaged, or eased with salve.

When you spread out your hands,
  I close my eyes to you;
Though you pray the more, I will not listen.
Your hands are full of blood! Wash yourselves clean!
Put away your misdeeds from before my eyes;
  cease doing evil; learn to do good.
Make justice your aim: redress the wronged,
  hear the orphan's plea, defend the widow.
Come now, let us set things right, says the Lord:
Though your sins be like scarlet, they may become white as snow;
Though they be crimson red, they may become white as wool.

115.   Is 5:1-7
Let me now sing of my friend, my friend's song concerning
  his vineyard.
My friend had a vineyard on a fertile hillside;
He spaded it, cleared it of stones, and planted the choicest vines;
Within it he built a watchtower, and hewed out a wine press.
Then he looked for the crop of grapes,
  but what it yielded was wild grapes.
Now, inhabitants of Jerusalem and men of Judah,
  judge between me and my vineyard:
What more was there to do for my vineyard
  that I had not done?

Why, when I looked for the crop of grapes,
    did it bring forth wild grapes?
Now, I will let you know what I mean to do to my vineyard:
Take away its hedge, give it to grazing,
    break through its wall, let it be trampled!
Yes, I will make it a ruin: it shall not be pruned or hoed,
    but overgrown with thorns and briers;
I will command the clouds not to send rain upon it.
The vineyard of the Lord of hosts is the house of Israel,
    and the men of Judah are his cherished plant;
He looked for judgment, but see, bloodshed!
    for justice, but hark, the outcry!

116. Is 43:22-28
Yet you did not call upon me, O Jacob,
    for you grew weary of me, O Israel.
You did not bring me sheep for your holocausts,
    nor honor me with your sacrifices.
I did not exact from you the service of offerings,
    nor weary you for frankincense.
You did not buy me sweet cane for money,
    nor fill me with the fat of your sacrifices;
Instead, you burdened me with your sins,
    and wearied me with your crimes.
It is I, I, who wipe out, for my own sake, your offenses;
    your sins I remember no more.
Would you have me remember, have us come to trial?
    Speak up, prove your innocence!
Your first father sinned; your spokesmen rebelled against me
Till I repudiated the holy gates, put Jacob under the ban,
    and exposed Israel to scorn.

117. Is 53:1-12 (pp. 22-23)
118. Is 55:1-11 (pp. 26-28)
119. Is 58:1-11 (pp. 99-100)
120. Is 59:1-4, 9-15
Lo, the hand of the Lord is not too short to save,
    nor his ear too dull to hear.
Rather, it is your crimes that separate you from your God,
It is your sins that make him hide his face
    so that he will not hear you.
For your hands are stained with blood,
    your fingers with guilt;
Your lips speak falsehood, and your tongue utters deceit.

No one brings suit justly, no one pleads truthfully;
They trust in emptiness and tell lies;
   they conceive mischief and bring forth malice.

That is why right is far from us and justice does not reach us.
We look for light, and lo, darkness;
   for brightness, but we walk in gloom!
Like blind men we grope along the wall,
   like people without eyes we feel our way.
We stumble at midday as at dusk,
   in Stygian darkness, like the dead.
We all growl like bears, like doves we moan without ceasing.
We look for right, but it is not there;
   for salvation, and it is far from us.
For our offenses before you are many,
   our sins bear witness against us.
Yes, our offenses are present to us,
   and our crimes we know:
Transgressing, and denying the Lord,
   turning back from following our God,
Threatening outrage, and apostasy,
   uttering words of falsehood the heart has conceived.
Right is repelled, and justice stands far off;
For truth stumbles in the public square,
   uprightness cannot enter.
Honesty is lacking, and the man who turns from
   evil is despoiled.

121. Jer 2:1-13
This word of the Lord came to me: Go, cry out this message
for Jerusalem to hear!

I remember the devotion of your youth,
   how you loved me as a bride,
Following me in the desert, in a land unsown.
Sacred to the Lord was Israel, the first fruits of his harvest;
Should anyone presume to partake of them,
   evil would befall him, says the Lord.
Listen to the word of the Lord, O house of Jacob!
   All you clans of the house of Israel, thus says the Lord:
What fault did your fathers find in me
   that they withdrew from me,
Went after empty idols, and became empty themselves?
They did not ask, "Where is the Lord
   who brought us up from the land of Egypt,

Who led us through the desert,
  through a land of wastes and gullies,
Through a land of drought and darkness,
  through a land which no one crosses, where no man dwells?"
When I brought you into the garden land
  to eat its goodly fruits,
You entered and defiled my land,
  you made my heritage loathsome.
The priests asked not "Where is the Lord?"
Those who dealt with the law knew me not;
  the shepherds rebelled against me.
The prophets prophesied by Baal,
  and went after useless idols.
Therefore will I yet accuse you, says the Lord,
  and even your children's children I will accuse.
Pass over to the coasts of the Kittim and see,
  send to Kedar and carefully inquire:
  Where has the like of this been done?
Does any other nation change its gods?—
  yet they are not gods at all!
But my people have changed their glory for useless things.
Be amazed at this, O heavens,
  and shudder with sheer horror, says the Lord.
Two evils have my people done:
  they have forsaken me, the source of living waters;
They have dug themselves cisterns,
  broken cisterns, that hold no water.

122. Jer 7:21-26

Thus says the Lord of hosts, the God of Israel: Heap your holocausts upon your sacrifices; eat up the flesh! In speaking to your fathers on the day I brought them out of the land of Egypt, I gave them no command concerning holocaust or sacrifice. This rather is what I commanded them: Listen to my voice; then I will be your God and you shall be my people. Walk in all the ways that I command you, so that you may prosper.

But they obeyed not, nor did they pay heed. They walked in the hardness of their evil hearts and turned their backs, not their faces, to me. From the day that your fathers left the land of Egypt even to this day, I have sent you untiringly all my servants the prophets. Yet they have not obeyed me nor paid heed; they have stiffened their necks and done worse than their fathers.

123. Ez 11:14-21

Thus the word of the Lord came to me: Son of man, it is about your kinsmen, your fellow exiles, and the whole house of Israel that the inhabitants of Jerusalem say, "They are far away from the Lord; to us the land of Israel has been given as our possession." Therefore say: Thus says the Lord God: Though I have removed them far among the nations and scattered them over foreign countries—and was for a while their only sanctuary in the countries to which they had gone—I will gather you from the nations and assemble you from the countries over which you have been scattered, and I will restore to you the land of Israel. They shall return to it and remove from it all its detestable abominations. I will give them a new heart and put a new spirit within them; I will remove the stony heart from their bodies, and replace it with a natural heart, so that they will live according to my statutes, and observe and carry out my ordinances; thus they shall be my people and I will be their God. But as for those whose hearts are devoted to their detestable abominations, I will bring down their conduct upon their heads, says the Lord God.

124. Ez 18:20-32 (pp. 23-24)

125. Ez 36:23-28

I will prove the holiness of my great name, profaned among the nations, in whose midst you have profaned it. Thus the nations shall know that I am the Lord, says the Lord God, when in their sight I prove my holiness through you. For I will take you away from among the nations, gather you from all the foreign lands, and bring you back to your own land. I will sprinkle clean water upon you to cleanse you from all your impurities, and from all your idols I will cleanse you. I will give you a new heart and place a new spirit within you, taking from your bodies your stony hearts and giving you natural hearts. I will put my spirit within you and make you live by my statutes, careful to observe my decrees. You shall live in the land I gave your fathers; you shall be my people, and I will be your God.

126. Hos 2:16-25

So I will allure her;
I will lead her into the desert and speak to her heart.
From there I will give her the vineyards she had,
and the valley of Achor as a door of hope.
She shall respond there as in the days of her youth,
when she came up from the land of Egypt.
On that day, says the Lord,

She shall call me "My husband," and never again "My baal."
Then will I remove from her mouth the names of the Baals,
  so that they shall no longer be invoked.
I will make a covenant for them on that day,
  with the beasts of the field,
With the birds of the air, and with the things that crawl on the
  ground.
Bow and sword and war I will destroy from the land,
  and I will let them take their rest in security.
I will espouse you to me forever:
  I will espouse you in right and in justice, in love and in mercy;
I will espouse you in fidelity,
  and you shall know the Lord.
On that day I will respond, says the Lord;
  I will respond to the heavens,
  and they shall respond to the earth;
The earth shall respond to the grain, and wine, and oil,
  and these shall respond to Jezreel.
I will sow him for myself in the land,
  and I will have pity on Lo-ruhama.
I will say to Lo-ammi, "You are my people,"
  and he shall say, "My God!"

127.   Hos 11:1-11
When Israel was a child I loved him,
  out of Egypt I called my son.
The more I called them, the farther they went from me,
Sacrificing to the Baals and burning incense to idols.
Yet it was I who taught Ephraim to walk,
  who took them in my arms;
I drew them with human cords, with bands of love!
I fostered them like one who raises an infant to his cheeks;
Yet, though I stooped to feed my child,
  they did not know that I was their healer.
He shall return to the land of Egypt,
and Assyria shall be his king;
The sword shall begin with his cities
  and end by consuming his solitudes.
Because they refused to repent,
  their own counsels shall devour them.
His people are in suspense about returning to him;
  and God, though in unison they cry out to him,
  shall not raise them up.
How could I give you up, O Ephraim,
  or deliver you up, O Israel?

How could I treat you as Admah, or make you like Zeboiim?
My heart is overwhelmed, my pity is stirred.
I will not give vent to my blazing anger,
   I will not destroy Ephraim again;
For I am God and not man, the Holy One present among you;
   I will not let the flames consume you.
They shall follow the Lord, who roars like a lion;
When he roars, his sons shall come frightened from the west,
Out of Egypt they shall come trembling, like sparrows,
   from the land of Assyria, like doves;
And I will resettle them in their homes, says the Lord.

128.   Hos 14:2-10
Return, O Israel, to the Lord, your God;
   you have collapsed through your guilt.
Take with you words, and return to the Lord;
Say to him, "Forgive all iniquity,
   and receive what is good, that we may render
   as offerings the bullocks from our stalls.
Assyria will not save us, nor shall we have horses to mount;
We shall say no more, 'Our god,' to the work of our hands;
   for in you the orphan finds compasion."
I will heal their defection, I will love them freely;
   for my wrath is turned away from them.
I will be like the dew for Israel: he shall blossom like the lily;
He shall strike root like the Lebanon cedar,
   and put forth his shoots.
His splendor shall be like the olive tree
   and his fragrance like the Lebanon cedar.
Again they shall dwell in his shade and raise grain;
They shall blossom like the vine,
   and his fame shall be like the wine of Lebanon.
Ephraim! What more has he to do with idols?
   I have humbled him, but I will prosper him.
"I am like a verdant cypress tree"—
   Because of me you bear fruit!
                              *   *   *

Let him who is wise understand these things;
   let him who is prudent know them.
Straight are the paths of the Lord,
   in them the just walk, but sinners stumble in them.

129. Jl 2:12-19 (pp. 28-29)
130. Mi 6:1-4, 6-8
   Hear, then, what the Lord says:
Arise, present your plea before the mountains,
   and let the hills hear your voice!
Hear, O mountains, the plea of the Lord,
   pay attention, O foundations of the earth!
For the Lord has a plea against his people,
   and he enters into trial with Israel.
O my people, what have I done to you,
   or how have I wearied you? Answer me!
For I brought you up from the land of Egypt,
   from the place of slavery I released you;
And I sent before you Moses, Aaron, and Miriam.

With what shall I come before the Lord,
   and bow before God most high?
Shall I come before him with holocausts,
   with calves a year old?
Will the Lord be pleased with thousands of rams,
   with myriad streams of oil?
Shall I give my first-born for my crime
   the fruit of my body for the sin of my soul?
You have been told, O man, what is good,
   and what the Lord requires of you:
Only to do the right and to love goodness,
   and to walk humbly with your God.

131. Ez 36:23-28 (p. 246)
132. Zec 1:1-6
   In the second year of Darius, in the eighth month, the word
of the Lord came to the prophet Zechariah, son of Berechiah,
son of Iddo: The Lord was indeed angry with your fathers. . . .
and say to them: Thus says the Lord of hosts: Return to me, says
the Lord of hosts, and I will return to you, says the Lord of hosts.
Be not like your fathers whom the former prophets warned:
Thus says the Lord of hosts: Turn from your evil ways and from
your wicked deeds. But they would not listen or pay attention
to me, says the Lord. Your fathers, where are they? And the
prophets, can they live forever? But my words and my decrees,
which I entrusted to my servants the prophets, did not these
overtake your fathers? Then they repented and admitted: "The
Lord of hosts has treated us according to our ways and deeds,
just as he had determined he would."

133. Ps 13

I

How long, O Lord? Will you utterly forget me?
  How long will you hide your face from me?
How long shall I harbor sorrow in my soul,
  grief in my heart day after day?
How long will my enemy triumph over me?
  Look, answer me, O Lord, my God!

II

Give light to my eyes that I may not sleep in death
  lest my enemy say, "I have overcome him";
Lest my foes rejoice at my downfall
  though I trusted in your kindness.
Let my heart rejoice in your salvation;
  let me sing of the Lord, "He has been good to me."

134. Ps 25

I

To you I lift up my soul,
  O Lord, my God.
In you I trust; let me not be put to shame,
  let not my enemies exult over me.
No one who waits for you shall be put to shame;
  those shall be put to shame who heedlessly break faith.
Your ways, O Lord, make known to me;
  teach me your paths,
Guide me in your truth and teach me,
  for you are God my savior,
  and for you I wait all the day.
Remember that your compassion, O Lord,
  and your kindness are from of old.
The sins of my youth and my frailties remember not;
  in your kindness remember me,
  because of your goodness, O Lord.

II

Good and upright is the Lord; thus he shows sinners the way.
He guides the humble to justice, he teaches the humble his way.
All the paths of the Lord are kindness and constancy
  toward those who keep his covenant and his decrees.
For your name's sake, O Lord,
  you will pardon my guilt, great as it is.
When a man fears the Lord,
  he shows him the way he should choose.

He abides in prosperity,
  and his descendants inherit the land.
The friendship of the Lord is with those who fear him,
  and his covenant, for their instruction.
My eyes are ever toward the Lord,
  for he will free my feet from the snare.

III
Look toward me, and have pity on me,
  for I am alone and afflicted.
Relieve the troubles of my heart,
  and bring me out of my distress.
Put an end to my affliction and my suffering,
  and take away all my sins.
Behold, my enemies are many,
  and they hate me violently.
Preserve my life, and rescue me;
  let me not be put to shame, for I take refuge in you.
Let integrity and uprightness preserve me,
  because I wait for you, O Lord.
Redeem Israel, O God, from all its distress!

135. Ps 31:1-6
I
In you, O Lord, I take refuge;
  let me never be put to shame.
In your justice rescue me,
  incline your ear to me, make haste to deliver me!
Be my rock of refuge, a stronghold to give me safety.
You are my rock and my fortress;
  for your name's sake you will lead and guide me.
You will free me from the snare they set for me,
  for you are my refuge.
Into your hands I commend my spirit;
  you will redeem me, O Lord, O faithful God.

136. Ps 32 (pp. 73-74)
137. Ps 36
I
Sin speaks to the wicked man in his heart;
  there is no dread of God before his eyes,
For he beguiles himself with the thought
  that his guilt will not be found out or hated.
The words of his mouth are empty and false;

he has ceased to understand how to do good.
He plans wickedness in his bed;
 he sets out on a way that is not good, with no repugnance
 for evil.

II

O Lord, your kindness reaches to heaven;
 your faithfulness, to the clouds.
Your justice is like the mountains of God;
 your judgments, like the mighty deep;
 man and beast you save, O Lord.
How precious is your kindness, O God!
 The children of men take refuge in the shadow of your wings.
They have their fill of the prime gifts of your house;
 from your delightful stream you give them to drink.
For with you is the fountain of life,
 and in your light we see light.

III

Keep up your kindness toward your friends,
 your just defense of the upright of heart.
Let not the foot of the proud overtake me
 nor the hand of the wicked disquiet me.
See how the evildoers have fallen;
 they are thrust down and cannot rise.

138. Ps 50:7-8, 14-23
"Hear, my people, and I will speak;
 Israel, I will testify against you;
 God, your God, am I.
Not for your sacrifices do I rebuke you,
 for your holocausts are before me always.

Offer to God praise as your sacrifice
 and fulfill your vows to the Most High;
Then call upon me in time of distress;
 I will rescue you, and you shall glorify me."
But to the wicked man God says: "Why do you recite my statutes,
 and profess my covenant with your mouth,
Though you hate discipline and cast my words behind you?
When you see a thief, you keep pace with him,
 and with adulterers you throw in your lot.
To your mouth you give free rein for evil,
 you harness your tongue to deceit.
You sit speaking against your brother;

against your mother's son you spread rumors.
When you do these things, shall I be deaf to it?
    Or do you think that I am like yourself?
    I will correct you by drawing them up before your eyes.
Consider this, you who forget God,
    lest I rend you and there be no one to rescue you.
He that offers praise as a sacrifice glorifies me;
    and to him that goes the right way I will show the
        salvation of God."

139.   Ps 51 (pp. 74-76)
140.   Ps 73
How good God is to the upright;
    the Lord, to those who are clean of heart!
But, as for me, I almost lost my balance;
    my feet all but slipped,
Because I was envious of the arrogant
    when I saw them prosper though they were wicked.

I

For they are in no pain;
    their bodies are sound and sleek;
They are free from the burdens of mortals,
    and are not afflicted like the rest of men.
So pride adorns them as a necklace;
    as a robe violence enwraps them.
Out of their crassness comes iniquity;
    their fancies overflow their hearts.
They scoff and speak evil;
    outrage from on high they threaten.
They set their mouthings in place of heaven,
    and their pronouncements roam the earth:
"So he brings his people to such a pass
    that they have not even water!"
And they say, "How does God know?"
    And, "Is there any knowledge in the Most High?"
Such, then, are the wicked;
    always carefree, while they increase in wealth.

II

Is it but in vain I have kept my heart clean
    and washed my hands as an innocent man?
For I suffer affliction day after day
    and chastisement with each new dawn.
Had I thought, "I will speak as they do,"

253

I had been false to the fellowship of your children.
Though I tried to understand this it seemed to me too difficult,
Till I entered the sanctuary of God
  and considered their final destiny.

III
You set them, indeed, on a slippery road;
  you hurl them down to ruin.
How suddenly they are made desolate!
  They are completely wasted away amid horrors.
As though they were the dream of one who had awakened,
    O Lord,
  so will you, when you arise, set at nought these phantoms.
Because my heart was embittered
  and my soul was pierced,
I was stupid and understood not;
  I was like a brute beast in your presence.

IV
Yet with you I shall always be;
  you have hold of my right hand;
With your counsel you guide me,
  and in the end you will receive me in glory.
Whom else have I in heaven?
And when I am with you, the earth delights me not.
Though my flesh and my heart waste away,
  God is the rock of my heart and my portion forever.
For indeed, they who withdraw from you perish;
  you destroy everyone who is unfaithful to you.
But for me, to be near God is my good;
  to make the Lord God my refuge.
I shall declare all your works
  in the gates of the daughter of Zion.

141. Ps 90
I
O Lord, you have been our refuge
  through all generations.
Before the mountains were begotten
  and the earth and the world were brought forth,
  from everlasting to everlasting you are God.
You turn man back to dust,
  saying, "Return, O children of men."

254

For a thousand years in your sight
  are as yesterday, now that it is past,
  or as a watch of the night.
You make an end of them in their sleep;
  the next morning they are like the changing grass,
Which at dawn springs up anew,
  but by evening wilts and fades.

II
Truly we are consumed by your anger,
  and by your wrath we are put to rout.
You have kept our iniquities before you,
  our hidden sins in the light of your scrutiny.
All our days have passed away in your indignation;
  we have spent our years like a sigh.
Seventy is the sum of our years,
  or eighty, if we are strong,
And most of them are fruitless toil,
  for they pass quickly and we drift away.
Who knows the fury of your anger
  or your indignation toward those who should fear you?

III
Teach us to number our days aright,
  that we may gain wisdom of heart.
Return, O Lord! How long?
  Have pity on your servants!
Fill us at daybreak with your kindness,
  that we may shout for joy and gladness all our days.
Make us glad, for the days when you afflicted us,
  for the years when we saw evil.
Let your work be seen by your servants
  and your glory by their children;
And may the gracious care of the Lord our God be ours;
  prosper the work of our hands for us!
  [Prosper the work of our hands!]

142. Ps 95
I
Come, let us sing joyfully to the Lord;
  let us acclaim the Rock of our salvation.
Let us greet him with thanksgiving;
  let us joyfully sing psalms to him.
For the Lord is a great God,
  and a great king above all gods;

In his hands are the depths of the earth,
    and the tops of the mountains are his.
His is the sea, for he has made it,
    and the dry land, which his hands have formed.

II

Come, let us bow down in worship;
    let us kneel before the Lord who made us.
For he is our God,
    and we are the people he shepherds, the flock he guides.

III

Oh, that today you would hear his voice:
    "Harden not your hearts as at Meribah,
    as in the day of Massah in the desert,
Where your fathers tempted me;
    they tested me though they had seen my works.
Forty years I loathed that generation,
    and I said: They are a people of erring heart,
    and they know not my ways.
Therefore I swore in my anger:
    They shall not enter into my rest."

143. Ps 119:1, 10-13, 15-16
Happy are they whose way is blameless,
    who walk in the law of the Lord.

With all my heart I seek you;
    let me not stray from your commands.
Within my heart I treasure your promise,
    that I may not sin against you.
Blessed are you, O Lord;
    teach me your statutes.
With my lips I declare
    all the ordinances of your mouth.
I will meditate on your precepts
    and consider your ways.
In your statutes I will delight;
    I will not forget your words.

144. Ps 123
I
To you I lift up my eyes
    who are enthroned in heaven.
Behold, as the eyes of servants

are on the hands of their masters,
As the eyes of a maid
   are on the hands of her mistress,
So are our eyes on the Lord, our God,
   till he have pity on us.

II

Have pity on us, O Lord, have pity on us,
   for we are more than sated with contempt;
Our souls are more than sated
   with the mockery of the arrogant,
   with the contempt of the proud.

145.   Ps. 130 (pp. 13-14)
146.   Ps. 139:1-18, 23-24

I

O Lord, you have probed me and you know me;
   you know when I sit and when I stand;
   you understand my thoughts from afar.
My journeys and my rest you scrutinize,
   with all my ways you are familiar.
Even before a word is on my tongue,
   behold, O Lord, you know the whole of it.
Behind me and before, you hem me in
   and rest your hand upon me.
Such knowledge is too wonderful for me;
   too lofty for me to attain.

II

Where can I go from your spirit?
   from your presence where can I flee?
If I go up to the heavens, you are there;
   if I sink to the nether world, you are present there.
If I take the wings of the dawn,
   if I settle at the farthest limits of the sea,
Even there your hand shall guide me
   and your right hand hold me fast.
If I say, "Surely the darkness shall hide me,
   and night shall be my light"—
For you darkness itself is not dark,
   and night shines as the day.
   [Darkness and light are the same.]

III

Truly you have formed my inmost being;
   you knit me in my mother's womb.
I give you thanks that I am fearfully, wonderfully made;
   wonderful are your works.
My soul also you knew full well;
   nor was my frame unknown to you
When I was made in secret,
   when I was fashioned in the depths of the earth.
Your eyes have seen my actions;
   in your book they are all written;
   my days were limited before one of them existed.
How weighty are your designs, O God;
   how vast the sum of them!
Were I to recount them, they would outnumber the sands;
   did I reach the end of them, I should still be with you.

Probe me, O God, and know my heart;
   try me, and know my thoughts;
See if my way is crooked,
   and lead me in the way of old.

     But now the justice of God has been manifested apart from
the law, even though both law and prophets bear witness to it—
that justice of God which works through faith in Jesus Christ for
all who believe. All men have sinned and are deprived of the
glory of God. All men are now undeservedly justified by the
gift of God, through the redemption wrought in Christ Jesus.
Through his blood, God made him the means of expiation for
all who believe. He did so to manifest his own justice, for the
sake of remitting sins committed in the past—to manifest his
justice in the present, by way of forbearance, so that he might be
just and might justify those who believe in Jesus.

154. Rm 13:8-14

Owe no debt to anyone except the debt that binds us to love
one another. He who loves his neighbor has fulfilled the law.
The commandments, "You shall not commit adultery; you shall
not murder; you shall not steal; you shall not covet," and any
other commandment there may be are all summed up in this,
"You shall love your neighbor as yourself." Love never does any
wrong to the neighbor, hence love is the fulfillment of the law.
Take care to do all these things, for you know the time in which
we are living. It is now the hour for you to wake from sleep,
for our salvation is closer than when we first accepted the faith.
The night is far spent; the day draws near. Let us cast off deeds
of darkness and put on the armor of light. Let us live honorably
as in daylight; not in carousing and drunkenness, not in sexual
excess and lust, not in quarreling and jealousy. Rather, put on
the Lord Jesus Christ and make no provision for the desires of
the flesh.

155. 2 Cor 5:17-21

This means that if anyone is in Christ, he is a new creation.
The old order has passed away; now all is new! All this has been
done by God, who has reconciled us to himself through Christ
and has given us the ministry of reconciliation. I mean that God,
in Christ, was reconciling the world to himself, not counting
men's transgressions against them, and that he has entrusted the
message of reconciliation to us. This makes us ambassadors for
Christ, God as it were appealing through us. We implore you,
in Christ's name: be reconciled to God! For our sakes God made
him who did not know sin, to be sin, so that in him we might
become the very holiness of God.

156.   Gal 5:16-24 (pp. 41-42)
157.   Eph 2:1-10 (pp. 88-89)
158.   Eph 4:1-3, 17-32 (pp. 89-90)
159.   Eph 5:1-14 (pp. 42-43)
160.   Eph 6:10-18 (p. 46)
161.   Col 3:1-10 (pp. 91-92)
162.   Heb 12:1-5

Therefore, since we for our part are surrounded by this
cloud of witnesses, let us lay aside every encumbrance of sin
which clings to us and persevere in running the race which lies
ahead; let us keep our eyes fixed on Jesus, who inspires and
perfects our faith. For the sake of the joy which lay before him
he endured the cross, heedless of his shame. He has taken his
seat at the right of the throne of God. Remember how he

endured the opposition of sinners; hence do not grow despondent
or abandon the struggle. In your fight against sin you have not yet
resisted to the point of shedding blood. Moreover, you have
forgotten the encouraging words addressed to you as sons:
"My sons, do not disdain the discipline of the Lord
    nor lose heart when he reproves you;
For whom the Lord loves, he disciplines;
    he scourges every son he receives."

163.   Jas 1:22-27 (p. 93)
164.   Jas 2:14-26 (pp. 93-94)
165.   Jas 3:1-12 (pp. 49-50)
166.   1 Pt 1:13-23

So gird the loins of your understanding; live soberly; set all
your hope on the gift to be conferred on you when Jesus Christ
appears. As obedient sons, do not yield to the desires that once
shaped you in your ignorance. Rather, become holy yourselves
in every aspect of your conduct, after the likeness of the holy
One who called you; remember, Scripture says, "Be holy, for I
am holy." In prayer you call upon a Father who judges each
one justly on the basis of his actions. Since this is so, conduct
yourselves reverently during your sojourn in a strange land.
Realize that you were delivered from the futile way of life your
fathers handed on to you, not by any diminishable sum of silver
or gold, but by Christ's blood beyond all price: the blood of a
spotless, unblemished lamb chosen before the world's foundation
and revealed for your sake in these last days. It is through him
that you are believers in God, the God who raised him from
the dead and gave him glory. Your faith and hope, then, are
centered in God. By obedience to the truth you have purified
yourselves for a genuine love of your brothers; therefore, love
one another constantly from the heart. Your rebirth has come,
not from a destructible but from an indestructible seed, through
the living and enduring word of God.

167.   2 Pt 1:3-11

That divine power of his has freely bestowed on us everything necessary for a life of genuine piety, through knowledge
of him who called us by his own glory and power. By virtue of
them he has bestowed on us the great and precious things he
promised, so that through these you who have fled a world
corrupted by lust might become sharers of the divine nature. This
is reason enough for you to make every effort to undergird your
virtue with faith, your discernment with virtue, and your self-
control with discernment; this self-control, in turn, should lead

to perseverance, and perseverance to piety, and piety to care
for your brother, and care for your brother, to love.

Qualities like these, made increasingly your own, are by no
means ineffectual; they bear fruit in true knowledge of our
Lord Jesus Christ. Any man who lacks these qualities is short-
sighted to the point of blindness. He forgets the cleansing of
his long-past sins. Be solicitous to make your call and election
permanent, brothers; surely those who do so will never be lost.
On the contrary, your entry into the everlasting kingdom of our
Lord and Savior Jesus Christ will be richly provided for.

168.   1 Jn 1:5-10; 2:1-2
Here, then, is the message
we have heard from him
and announce to you:
that God is light;
in him there is no darkness.
If we say, "We have fellowship with him,"
while continuing to walk in darkness,
we are liars and do not act in truth.

But if we walk in light, as he is in the light,
we have fellowship with one another,
and the blood of his Son Jesus cleanses us from all sin.
If we say, "We are free of the guilt of sin,"
we deceive ourselves; the truth is not to be found in us.
But if we acknowledge our sins,
he who is just can be trusted
to forgive our sins
and cleanse us from every wrong.
If we say, "We have never sinned,"
we make him a liar
and his word finds no place in us.

My little ones,
I am writing this to keep you from sin.
But if anyone should sin,
we have, in the presence of the Father,
Jesus Christ, an intercessor who is just.
He is an offering for our sins,
and not for our sins only,
but for those of the whole world.

169. 1 Jn 2:3-11
The way we can be sure of our knowledge of him
is to keep his commandments.
The man who claims, "I have known him,"
without keeping his commandments,
is a liar; in such a one there is no truth.
But whoever keeps his word,
truly has the love of God been made perfect in him.
The way we can be sure we are in union with him
is for the man who claims to abide in him
to conduct himself just as he did.
Dearly beloved,
it is no new commandment that I write to you,
but an old one which you had from the start.
The commandment, now old, is the word you have already heard.
On second thought, the commandment that I write you is new,
as it is realized in him and you,
for the darkness is over
and the real light begins to shine.
The man who claims to be in light,
hating his brother all the while, is in darkness even now.
The man who continues in the light
is the one who loves his brother;
there is nothing in him to cause a fall.
But the man who hates his brother is in darkness.
He walks in shadows,
not knowing where he is going,
since the dark has blinded his eyes.

170. 1 Jn 3:1-24 (pp. 94-96)
171. 1 Jn 4:16-21 (pp. 96-98)
172. Rv 2:1-5
   "To the presiding spirit of the church in Ephesus, write this:
   " 'The One who holds the seven stars in his right hand and
walks among the seven lampstands of gold has this to say:
I know your deeds, your labors, and your patient endurance.
I know you cannot tolerate wicked men; you have tested those
self-styled apostles who are nothing of the sort, and discovered
that they are impostors. You are patient and endure hardship
for my cause. Moreover, you do not become discouraged. I
hold this against you, though: you have turned aside from your
early love. Keep firmly in mind the heights from which you have
fallen. Repent, and return to your former deeds. If you do not
repent I will come to you and remove your lampstand from its

262

place. But you have this much in your favor: you detest the practices of the Nicolaitans, just as I do.' "

173. Rv 3:14-22

"To the presiding spirit of the church in Laodicea, write this:

" 'The Amen, the faithful Witness and true, the Source of God's creation, has this to say: I know your deeds; I know you are neither hot nor cold. How I wish you were one or the other—hot or cold! But because you are lukewarm, neither hot nor cold, I will spew you out of my mouth! You keep saying, "I am so rich and secure that I want for nothing." Little do you realize how wretched you are, how pitiable and poor, how blind and naked! Take my advice. Buy from me gold refined by fire if you would be truly rich. Buy white garments in which to be clothed, if the shame of your nakedness is to be covered. Buy ointment to smear on your eyes, if you would see once more. Whoever is dear to me I reprove and chastise. Be earnest about it, therefore. Repent!

" 'Here I stand, knocking at the door. If anyone hears me calling and opens the door, I will enter his house and have supper with him, and he with me. I will give the victor the right to sit with me on my throne, as I myself won the victory and took my seat beside my Father on his throne.

" 'Let him who has ears heed the Spirit's word to the churches.' "

174. Rv 20:11-15

Next I saw a large white throne and the One who sat on it. The earth and the sky fled from his presence until they could no longer be seen. I saw the dead, the great and the lowly, standing before the throne. Lastly, among the scrolls, the book of the living was opened. The dead were judged according to their conduct as recorded on the scrolls. The sea gave up its dead; then death and the nether world gave up their dead. Each person was judged according to his conduct. Then death and the nether world were hurled into the pool of fire, which is the second death; anyone whose name was not found inscribed in the book of the living was hurled into this pool of fire.

175. Rv 21:1-8

Then I saw new heavens and a new earth. The former heavens and the former earth had passed away, and the sea was no longer. I also saw a new Jerusalem, the holy city, coming down out of heaven from God, beautiful as a bride prepared to meet her husband. I heard a loud voice from the throne cry out:

"This is God's dwelling among men. He shall dwell with them and they shall be his people and he shall be their God who is always with them. He shall wipe every tear from their eyes, and there shall be no more death or mourning, crying out or pain, for the former world has passed away."

The One who sat on the throne said to me, "See, I make all things new!" Then he said, "Write these matters down, for the words are trustworthy and true!" He went on to say: "These words are already fulfilled! I am the Alpha and the Omega, the Beginning and the End. To anyone who thirsts I will give to drink without cost from the spring of lifegiving water. He who wins the victory shall inherit these gifts; I will be his God and he shall be my son. As for the cowards and traitors to the faith, the depraved and murderers, the fornicators and sorcerers, the idol-worshipers and deceivers of every sort—their lot is the fiery pool of burning sulphur, the second death!"

176. Mt 3:1-12

When John the Baptizer made his appearance as a preacher in the desert of Judea, this was his theme: "Reform your lives! The reign of God is at hand." It was of him that the prophet Isaiah had spoken when he said:

"A herald's voice in the desert:
'Prepare the way of the Lord, make straight his paths.' "

John was clothed in a garment of camel's hair, and wore a leather belt around his waist. Grasshoppers and wild honey were his food. At that time Jerusalem, all Judea, and the whole region around the Jordan were going out to him. They were being baptized by him in the Jordan River as they confessed their sins.

When he saw that many of the Pharisees and Sadducees were stepping forward for this bath, he said to them: "You brood of vipers! Who told you to flee from the wrath to come? Give some evidence that you mean to reform. Do not pride yourselves on the claim, 'Abraham is our father.' I tell you, God can raise up children to Abraham from these very stones. Even now the ax is laid to the root of the tree. Every tree that is not fruitful will be cut down and thrown into the fire. I baptize you in water for the sake of reform, but the one who will follow me is more powerful than I. I am not even fit to carry his sandals. He it is who will baptize you in the Holy Spirit and fire. His winnowing-fan is in his hand. He will clear the threshing floor and gather his grain into the barn, but the chaff he will burn in unquenchable fire."

177. Mt 4:12-17

When Jesus heard that John had been arrested, he withdrew
to Galilee. He left Nazareth and went down to live in Caper-
naum by the sea near the territory of Zebulun and Naphtali,
to fulfill what had been said through Isaiah the prophet:

"Land of Zebulun, land of Naphtali
along the sea beyond the Jordan,
heathen Galilee: a people living in darkness
has seen a great light.
On those who inhabit a land overshadowed by death,
light has arisen."

From that time on Jesus began to proclaim this theme: "Reform
your lives! The kingdom of heaven is at hand."

178. Mt 5:1-12 (pp. 78-79)
179. Mt 5:13-16

"You are the salt of the earth. But what if salt goes flat?
How can you restore its flavor? Then it is good for nothing but to
be thrown out and trampled underfoot.

"You are the light of the world. A city set on a hill cannot
be hidden. Men do not light a lamp and then put it under a
bushel basket. They set it on a stand where it gives light to all
in the house. In the same way, your light must shine before men
so that they may see goodness in your acts and give praise to
your heavenly Father."

180. Mt 5:17-47 (See also pp. 43-45, 50-51)

"Do not think that I have come to abolish the law and the
prophets. I have come, not to abolish them, but to fulfill them.
Of this much I assure you: until heaven and earth pass away,
not the smallest letter of the law, not the smallest part of a
letter, shall be done away with until it all comes true. That is
why whoever breaks the least significant of these commands and
teaches others to do so shall be called least in the kingdom
of God. Whoever fulfills and teaches these commands shall
be great in the kingdom of God. I tell you, unless your holiness
surpasses that of the scribes and Pharisees you shall not enter
the kingdom of God."

Against Anger

"You have heard the commandment imposed on your forefathers, 'You shall not commit murder; every murderer shall be
liable to judgment.' What I say to you is: everyone who grows

265

angry with his brother shall be liable to judgment; any man who uses abusive language toward his brother shall be answerable to the Sanhedrin, and if he holds him in contempt he risks the fires of Gehenna. If you bring your gift to the altar and there recall that your brother has anything against you, leave your gift at the altar, go first to be reconciled with your brother, and then come and offer your gift. Lose no time; settle with your opponent while on your way to court with him. Otherwise your opponent may hand you over to the judge, who will hand you over to the guard, who will throw you into prison. I warn you, you will not be released until you have paid the last penny."

Occasions of Impurity

"You have heard the commandment, 'You shall not commit adultery.' What I say to you is: anyone who looks lustfully at a woman has already committed adultery with her in his thoughts. If your right eye is your trouble, gouge it out and throw it away! Better to lose part of your body than to have it all cast into Gehenna. Again, if your right hand is your trouble cut it off and throw it away! Better to lose part of your body than to have it all cast into Gehenna.

"It was also said, 'Whenever a man divorces his wife, he must give her a decree of divorce.' What I say to you is: everyone who divorces his wife—lewd conduct is a separate case—forces her to commit adultery. The man who marries a divorced woman likewise commits adultery."

On Oaths

"You have heard the commandment imposed on your forefathers, 'Do not take a false oath; rather, make good to the Lord all your pledges.' What I tell you is: do not swear at all. Do not swear by heaven (it is God's throne), nor by the earth (it is his footstool), nor by Jerusalem (it is the city of the great King); do not swear by your head (you cannot make a single hair white or black). Say 'Yes' when you mean 'Yes' and 'No' when you mean 'No.' Anything beyond that is from the evil one."

New Law of Retaliation

"You have heard the commandment, 'An eye for an eye, a tooth for a tooth.' But what I say to you is: offer no resistance to injury. When a person strikes you on the right cheek, turn and offer him the other. If anyone wants to go to law over your shirt, hand him your coat as well. Should anyone press you into service for one mile, go with him two miles. Give to the man who begs from you. Do not turn your back on the borrower."

Love of Enemies

"You have heard the commandment, 'You shall love your countryman but hate your enemy.' My command to you is: love your enemies, pray for your persecutors. This will prove that you are sons of your heavenly Father, for his sun rises on the bad and the good, he rains on the just and the unjust. If you love those who love you, what merit is there in that? Do not tax collectors do as much? And if you greet your brothers only, what is so praiseworthy about that? Do not pagans do as much?"

181. Mt 9:1-8
Then he reentered the boat, made the crossing, and came back to his own town. There the people at once brought to him a paralyzed man lying on a mat. When Jesus saw their faith he said to the paralytic, "Have courage, son, your sins are forgiven." At that some of the scribes said to themselves, "The man blasphemes." Jesus was aware of what they were thinking and said: "Why do you harbor evil thoughts? Which is less trouble to say, 'Your sins are forgiven' or 'Stand up and walk'? To help you realize that the Son of Man has authority on earth to forgive sins"— he then said to the paralyzed man— "Stand up! Roll up your mat, and go home." The man stood up and went toward his home. At the sight, a feeling of awe came over the crowd, and they praised God for giving such authority to men.

186. Mt 26:69-75
Peter was sitting in the courtyard when one of the serving girls came over to him and said, "You too were with Jesus the Galilean." He denied it in front of everyone: "I do not know what you are talking about!" When he went out to the gate another girl saw him and said to those nearby, "This man was with Jesus the Nazorean." Again he denied it with an oath: "I do not know the man!" A little while later some bystanders came over to Peter and said, "You are certainly one of them! Even your accent gives you away!" At that he began cursing, and swore, "I do not even know the man!" Just then a cock began to crow and Peter remembered the prediction Jesus had made: "Before the cock crows, you will deny me three times." He went out and began to weep bitterly.

187. Mk 12:28-34 (p. 32)
188. Lk 7:36-50 (pp. 16-17)
189. Lk 13:1-5

At that time, some were present who told him about the Galileans whose blood Pilate had mixed with their sacrifices. He said in reply: "Do you think that these Galileans were the greatest sinners in Galilee just because they suffered this? By no means! But I tell you, you will all come to the same end unless you reform. Or take those eighteen who were killed by a falling tower in Siloam. Do you think they were more guilty than anyone else who lived in Jerusalem? Certainly not! But I tell you, you will all come to the same end unless you reform."

190. Lk 15:1-10 (pp. 17, 18)
191. Lk 5:11-32 (pp. 18-19)
192. Lk 17:1-4

He said to his disciples: "Scandals will inevitably arise, but woe to him through whom they come. He would be better off thrown into the sea with a millstone around his neck than giving scandal to one of these little ones.

"Be on your guard. If your brother does wrong, correct him; if he repents, forgive him. If he sins against you seven times a day, and seven times a day turns back to you saying, 'I am sorry,' forgive him."

193. Lk 18:9-14 (p. 49)
194. Lk 19:1-10 (p. 20)
195. Lk 23:39-43

One of the criminals hanging in crucifixion blasphemed him: "Aren't you the Messiah? Then save yourself and us." But the other one rebuked him: "Have you no fear of God, seeing you are under the same sentence? We deserve it, after all. We are only paying the price for what we've done, but this man has done nothing wrong." He then said, "Jesus, remember me when you enter upon your reign." And Jesus replied, "I assure you: this day you will be with me in paradise."

196. Jn 8:1-11 (pp. 20-21)
197. Jn 8:31-36

Jesus then went on to say to those Jews who believed in him:
"If you live according to my teaching,
  you are truly my disciples;
  then you will know the truth,
  and the truth will set you free."

"We are descendants of Abraham," was their answer. "Never

have we been slaves to anyone. What do you mean by saying,
'You will be free'?" Jesus answered them:
"I give you my assurance,
   everyone who lives in sin is the slave of sin.
(No slave has a permanent place in the family,
but the son has a place there forever.)
That is why, if the son frees you, you will really be free.

198.   Jn 15:1-8 (pp. 82-83)
199.   Jn 15:9-14 (pp. 83-84)
200.   Jn 19:13-37
   Pilate heard what they were saying, then brought Jesus outside
and took a seat on a judge's bench at the place called the Stone
Pavement—Gabbatha in Hebrew. (It was the Preparation Day for
Passover, and the hour was about noon.) He said to the Jews,
"Look at your king!" At this they shouted, "Away with him!
Away with him! Crucify him!" "What!" Pilate exclaimed. "Shall
I crucify your king?" The chief priests replied, "We have no king
but Caesar." In the end, Pilate handed Jesus over to be crucified.

Jesus was led away, and carrying the cross by himself, went
out to what is called the Place of the Skull (in Hebrew, Golgotha).
There they crucified him, and two others with him: one on either
side, Jesus in the middle. Pilate had an inscription placed on the
cross which read,

JESUS THE NAZOREAN
THE KING OF THE JEWS

   This inscription, in Hebrew, Latin, and Greek, was read by
many of the Jews, since the place where Jesus was crucified was
near the city. The chief priests of the Jews tried to tell Pilate,
"You should not have written, 'The King of the Jews.' Write instead, 'This man claimed to be King of the Jews.' " Pilate
answered, "What I have written, I have written."
   After the soldiers had crucified Jesus they took his garments
and divided them four ways, one for each soldier. There was
also his tunic, but his tunic was woven in one piece from
top to bottom and had no seam. They said to each other, "We
should not tear it. Let us throw dice to see who gets it." (The
purpose of this was to have the Scripture fulfilled:
"They divided my garments among them;
   for my clothing they cast lots.")
And this was what the soldiers did.
   Near the cross of Jesus there stood his mother, his mother's

sister, Mary the wife of Clopas, and Mary Magdalene. Seeing his mother there with the disciple whom he loved, Jesus said to his mother, "Woman, there is your son." In turn he said to the disciple, "There is your mother." From that hour onward, the disciple took her into his care.

After that, Jesus, realizing that everything was not finished, said to fulfill the Scripture, "I am thirsty." There was a jar there, full of common wine. They stuck a sponge soaked in this wine on some hyssop and raised it to his lips. When Jesus took the wine, he said, "Now it is finished." Then he bowed his head, and delivered over his spirit.

Since it was the Preparation Day the Jews did not want to have the bodies left on the cross during the sabbath, for that sabbath was a solemn feast day. They asked Pilate that the legs be broken and the bodies be taken away. Accordingly, the soldiers came and broke the legs of the men crucified with Jesus, first of the one, then of the other. When they came to Jesus and saw that he was already dead, they did not break his legs. One of the soldiers thrust a lance into his side, and immediately blood and water flowed out. (This testimony has been given by an eyewitness, and his testimony is true. He tells what he knows is true, so that you may believe.) These events took place for the fulfillment of Scripture:

"Break none of his bones."

There is still another Scripture passage which says:

"They shall look on him whom they have pierced."

201. Jn 20:19-23 (p. 21)

270